Eurasian Mission

ALEXANDER DUGIN

EURASIAN MISSON

AN INTRODUCTION TO NEO-EURASIANISM

ARKTOS
2014

First edition published in 2014 by Arktos Media Ltd.

Copyright © 2014 by Arktos Media Ltd.

Printed in the United Kingdom.

ISBN 978-1-910524-24-4

BIC CLASSIFICATION
Russia (1DVUA)
Geopolitics (JPSL)
Political science and theory (JPA)

EDITOR
John B. Morgan IV

LAYOUT AND COVER DESIGN
Tor Westman

ARKTOS MEDIA LTD.
www.arktos.com

CONTENTS

Editor's Note

The following texts were selected by me in collaboration with Prof. Dugin from many different sources as giving an overview of the ideology of neo-Eurasianism as propagated by the International Eurasian Movement (IEM) in Russia today. Chapters 1 through 8 were originally published as a booklet in Russia in 2005. Chapters 9 and 11 were written in 2011, chapters 10 and 12 in 2012, and chapters 13 and 14 in 2014. Chapter 15 was published as a booklet by the IEM in Russia in 2012. Chapter 16 was compiled by me from various informal statements that Prof. Dugin made on his Facebook wall in 2012 and 2013. Chapter 17 is the transcript of an interview with Prof. Dugin that was conducted in February 2012, shortly before the re-election of Vladimir Putin. The Introduction is original to this volume.

Some of these texts were originally written in English, and some were translated anonymously by volunteers from the International Eurasian Movement — all were re-edited by me. To these volunteers I give my thanks.

Those who are interested in learning more about neo-Eurasianism can visit the official Fourth Political Theory Website at www.4pt.su.

JOHN B. MORGAN
November 24, 2014

Introduction

Eurasianism and the Fourth Political Theory

Eurasianism as structuralism

First of all, Eurasianism is a philosophy, and as all true philosophy it implicitly contains a political perspective, an approach to history and the possibility of being transformed into an ideology. Eurasianism as a philosophy is based on structural analysis and it is not a coincidence that the founder of Eurasianism, Count Nikolai Trubetzkoy, was a leading figure in structuralist linguistics. Eurasianism is a type of structuralism with the accent placed on the multiplicity and synchronicity of structures. The structure is viewed as a whole that is something much more than the sum of its parts. This is the rule of Eurasianism. It is holism dealing with organic, structural entities.

The primary concern of Eurasianist philosophy is civilization. There are different civilizations, not only one. Each of them has its own structure that defines the elements of which it consists, and which gives them meaning and coherence. We cannot apply the rules and structure we find in one such structure to those we find in other civilization — not in a diachronic or a synchronic way. Each civilizational structure possesses its own sense of time (*la durée*) and its own space. They are thus incomparable with one another. Every human society belongs to a particular civilization and should be studied only in accordance with its own criteria. This brings us to the starting point of modern anthropology, which began with Franz Boaz and Marcel Mauss, which insists on the plurality of human societies in the absence of any universal pattern. It is therefore no mere coincidence that Claude Lévi-Strauss, the well-known father of structural anthropology, studied under Roman Jakobson in the United States. Jakobson had been a colleague and friend of Trubetzkoy.

The plurality of human societies, each one of which represents a specific kind of semantic structure that is entirely unique and incomparable with any other, is the basis of Eurasian philosophy in general.

Eurasianism as hermeneutical tool

This principle was applied by the Eurasianists to various fields, including Russian history, geopolitics, sociology, international relations, cultural studies, political science, and so on. In any field the uniqueness of Russian civilization in comparison with all others, Western and well as Eastern, was affirmed and defended. Thus, Eurasianists view Western, European civilization as one concrete structure with its own understanding of time, space, history, human nature, values and goals. But there are other civilizations, namely Asian, African, Latin American and Russian. Russian civilization possesses some of the same features as Europe and some of the features of Asian culture (above all of the Turanian type), representing an organic synthesis of the two, and cannot therefore be reduced to the mere sum of its Western and Eastern elements. Rather it has an original identity.

The structural method caused the Eurasianists to begin to study this Russian civilization as an organic whole with its own semantics, which revealed the nature of its identity in its implicit way of understanding history, religion, normative politics, culture, strategy, and so on. But in order to conduct such a study in a truly structural way they were obliged to radically reject Western pretensions to universality, thus deconstructing Western universalism, ethnocentrism and its implicit cultural imperialism. Since the nature of Russian civilization is not Western, it should be defined beyond the "self-evident" principles taken for granted in European modernity, such as progress, linear time, homogeneous space, materialistic physics, capitalism as the universal destiny of social development, and so on. The term Eurasia, which could also be expressed as Russia-Eurasia, was introduced in order to define a clear line of demarcation between the two civilizations: the European, which was judged to be essentially a purely local phenomenon historically and geographically, and the Eurasian one. From this starting point, two schools emerged: the radical critics of Western universalism and eurocentrism (their position being formulated in Trubetzkoy's book *Europe and Mankind*, in which Europe is portrayed as being opposed to humanity as a whole in a way that is similar to Toynbee's duality of "the West and the rest"), and those who dealt with the independent Russian-Eurasian structure taken as a key for deciphering Russian history and as a means of creating a normative project for the Eurasian future — a Eurasian project.

The interpretations and projects of the Eurasianists

The Eurasian project was developed in the form of a political philosophy on the basis of the multipolarity of civilizations, anti-imperialism, anti-modernism and on the structure of Russia itself. This last was defined in terms of the principles of the Slavophiles, along with the important addition of a positive evaluation of the cultural elements which had been borrowed by the Russians from Asiatic societies beginning with the period of the Mongols. Indeed, one of the most important books of the Eurasianist movement, also written by Trubetzkoy, was called *The Legacy of Genghis Khan*. Therefore for the Eurasianists the West was in the wrong — a purely regional phenomenon pretending to universal status via imperialism; thus it follows that modernity, which was also a Western phenomenon, is also entirely a product of this locale and is inherently imperialistic. Russian history was considered as the struggle of Eurasian civilization against the West, and in the last centuries also as the struggle against modernity. Russia's Eurasian future should be built in a form that corresponds to the specificity of Russia's structure and in accordance with its values and basic beliefs. The Eurasianists proposed to take and affirm these qualities as its norms. They said "no" to progress. They saw social development as a cycle, not in terms of capitalist notions of development. They called for an organic, agricultural economy, not materialism, and for ideacracy (the power of ideas). They also said "no" to democracy, favoring popular monarchy. They rejected the notion of purely individualistic, superficial liberty, and advocated for social responsibility and spiritual, inner freedom.

The Eurasianists identified Russian-Eurasian structures within Bolshevism, but only in a very perverted and Westernized form (Marxism). They viewed the October Revolution of 1917 as more of an eschatological, messianic revolt than as a transition from a capitalist phase to a socialist one. The Eurasianists foresaw the inner transmutation of Bolshevism, which would bring about its metamorphosis into a Leftist Eurasianism and bring about a future return to the Christian Faith, to monarchy and to a pre-modern type of agricultural economy.

Their short-term expectations for the evolution of Eurasianism proved to be incorrect but were later realized in the 1980s, long after the extinction of the Eurasianist movement that had existed as a part of the White émigré movement following the October Revolution. Looking back from a time when most of their analyses have been confirmed, we have adopted their heritage as our own and thus commenced the second wave of Eurasianism: neo-Eurasianism.

Neo-Eurasianism: new features

Neo-Eurasianism, as well as early Eurasianism, was conceived by us from the outset as a Russian form of Third Way ideology belonging to the same philosophical family as the German Conservative Revolution. We therefore accepted it as a particularly Russian paradigm of a broad anti-modern philosophical and political tendency, akin to traditionalism or the Third Position. Left Eurasianism was represented by National Bolshevism.

An important confirmation of the relevance of Eurasianism to politics can be found in the way in which geopolitical thinking is conceived in dualistic terms, such as thalassocracy vs. tellurocracy or Atlanticism vs. Eurasianism. This coincides perfectly with the primary way that the first Eurasianists framed things in their *Weltanschauung*. Likewise, the Eurasianist Nikolai Alexeyev was the first scholar in Russia to cite René Guénon. Also, Eurasian criticism of modernity and eurocentrism was very close to the spirit of the European New Right as represented by Alain de Benoist. Neo-eurasianism was thus enriched by new themes: traditionalism, geopolitics, Carl Schmitt, Martin Heidegger, the Conservative Revolution, structuralism, anthropology, and so on.

In the early 1990s neo-Eurasianism was an integral part of the larger patriotic and anti-liberal movement (those in the opposition who represented a synthesis of the Left and the Right). After that, the Eurasianists became the core of the National Bolshevist movement. It wasn't until the late 1990s that an independent neo-Eurasianist movement, with its own political program, was formed. It based itself not only on older sources but also on new elements taken from Western anti-modern sources, including some from the school of postmodernism. In early 2000 it gained some level of social recognition and received its first positive responses from within the political circles around Vladimir Putin.

The Fourth Political Theory

The last important ideological shift in the philosophy of neo-Eurasianism occurred in 2007–2008, when the basic principles of the Fourth Political Theory were laid down. That was the moment of the resolute and irreversible step from Eurasianism as a Russian version of the Third Position to the Fourth Position. This was a continuation of Eurasianist ideas — still consisting of anti-liberalism, anti-modernism, anti-eurocentrism, the structuralist approach, and multipolarity — but instead of it being a creative synthesis of the anti-liberal (socialist) Right with the identitarian (non-dogmatic, or Sorelian for example) Left, it began to move in a direction taking it beyond all the varieties of political modernity. This included transcending the Third Position, or rather the mixture of the far Left with far Right (National Bolshevism). The idea behind this was to create the normative for the future, completely removed from any modern political tendency — beyond liberalism, Communism and fascism.

The Fourth Political Theory has begun, little by little, to take shape by overcoming the logic and principles of the Third Way, instead inviting those who consider it to freely affirm unmodern and non-Western structures as a valid foundation for a normative and sovereign civilization. The philosophical basis for the total destruction of modernity was laid by Heideggerian philosophy, which annihilates all of the modern philosophical concepts: subject, object, reality, time, space, technics, the individual, and so on. Some people, as for example the Brazilian philosopher Flavia Virginia, refer to this as "*Dasein* politics."

In the field of international relations, the theory of the multipolar world was recently elaborated by Eurasianists. Besides these geopolitical works, studies have been conducted in many other fields, such as ethnosociology, the sociology of imagination, noology, neo-traditionalism (based on the theme of the Radical Subject), an approach to an original Russian phenomenological philosophy, archeomodern studies, and so on. The amount and quality of such works created within the framework of the Fourth Political Theory have been sufficient to carve out a niche for it that is independent from both Eurasianism and neo-Eurasianism, but which continues in the same profound lines of forces. We could therefore consider the Fourth Political Theory as developing out of and as a continuation of Eurasianism in which Eurasianism represents its basic paradigm and starting point. It is theoretically possible to study the Fourth Political Theory without any knowledge of Eurasianism, but in order to understand its principles more deeply, familiarity with Eurasianism is desirable.

Looking at how things have developed, we can now recognize that Eurasianism is a kind of preparation for the Fourth Political Theory: the first stage leading to it. But at the same time, Eurasianism represents a coherent and self-sufficient philosophy and *Weltanschauung* based on this philosophy, and is thus a subject worth studying in its own right, apart from the more complicated and detailed domain of the Fourth Political Theory.

An introduction to Eurasianism

In this book we have gathered together various texts related to both Eurasianism and neo-Eurasianism. We hope they can serve as an introduction to more detailed studies. Until recently not much of this work was available in the English language, although Arktos has now published my books *The Fourth Political Theory* in 2012 and *Putin vs Putin* in 2014, and Washington Summit Publishers has issued *Martin Heidegger: The Philosophy of Another Beginning* in 2014. Arktos plans many more translations of my works in the near future.

Eurasianism can be applied to the field of geopolitics, where it represents the definitive summation of the perspective of the civilizations of the Land, as opposed to that of the civilizations of the Sea, the latter of which is the point of view of the Atlanticist politics of the United States at present and of its geopolitical strategic thinkers, such as Zbigniew Brzezinski. Several books detailing Eurasianist geopolitics have already been published, from my book *The Foundations of Geopolitics*, first issued in 1997, up to my recent and very detailed books *Geopolitika* (2012) and *The Geopolitics of Contemporary Russia* (2013). Translations of some of these books are being prepared by Arktos. I also published a manual of international relations in 2013. Geopolitical and strategic studies of this sort are now abundant in Russia and elsewhere.

Eurasianism has a secure place in the field of Russian history, developing along the line of George Vernadsky, the prominent Russian Eurasian historicist, and Lev Gumilev, the famous Russian Eurasianist ethnnologist. Eurasianism can be very useful for making accurate political analyses of the political situation in Russia, particularly for understanding the Putin phenomenon and his drive to create a Eurasian Union in the post-Soviet space.

In the broader sense, Eurasianism can be considered as a form of continental-ism for the project of the creation of a European-Russian common space — the Greater Europe stretching from Lisbon to Vladivostok, as declared by Vladimir Putin (who adopted the concept that had first been propagated by Jean Thiriart). Beyond this more localized project, Eurasianism advocates for multipolarity, representing an alternative to unipolar globalization and the neo-colonial Westernization that has adopted such forms as the BRICS (Brazil, Russia, India, China, and South Africa) accords.

Eurasianism can be very useful for those who are searching to understand the nature of the world we are living in — its challenges, its limits, and its paradigms, as well as its open and hidden agendas, its choices, and its alternatives. Above all it is an absolute necessity for anyone who wants to understand the true nature of Russia — its profound identity and its structures — past, present, or future.

EURASIANISM

Milestones of Eurasianism

A Historical and Conceptual Introduction to Eurasianism

Eurasianism[1] is an ideological and social-political current born within the environment of the first wave of Russian emigration, unified by the concept of Russian culture as a non-European phenomenon, and presenting — among the various cultures of the world — an original combination of Western and Eastern features; as a consequence, Russian culture belongs to both East and West, and at the same time cannot be reduced either to the former nor to the latter.

The founders of Eurasianism were:

✳ Nikolai S. Trubetzkoy (1890–1938), philologist and linguist.

✳ Pyotr N. Savitsky (1895–1965), geographer and economist.

✳ Georges V. Florovsky (1893–1979), historian of culture, theologian and patriot.

✳ George V. Vernadsky (1887–1973), historian and geopolitician.

✳ Nikolai N. Alexeyev (1879–1964), jurist and politologist.

✳ V. N. Ilin, historian of culture, literary scholar and theologian.

---

1   Eurasianism, in its broadest meaning, is a basic geopolitical term which seeks to understand the entire world from the historical and geographical point of view, excluding the Western sector of world civilization. It also attempts an understand of the world from the military-strategic point of view, specifically in terms of those countries that do not approve of the expansionist policies of the United States and their NATO partners. In terms of culture, it desires the preservation and development of organic national, ethnic and religious traditions; and from the social point of view, it embraces all the various forms of economic life and efforts toward the "socially just society."

Eurasianism's main value consisted of ideas born out of the depth of the tradition of Russian history and statehood. Eurasianism viewed Russian culture not as simply a component of European civilization, but also as an original civilization, encompassing the experience not only of the West but also — to the same extent — of the East. The Russian people, from this perspective, must not be placed either among the European nor among the Asian peoples; it belongs to a completely unique Eurasian community. Such originality in Russian culture and statehood (displaying European as well as Asian features) also defines the distinct historical path of Russia and of her national and state program, which does not coincide with that of the Western-European tradition.

Foundations

Civilization concept

The Roman-German civilization has worked out its own system of principles and values and promoted it to the rank of a universal system. This Roman-German system has been imposed on other peoples and cultures by force and ruse. The Western spiritual and material colonization of the rest of mankind is a negative phenomenon. Every people and culture has its own intrinsic right to evolve according to its own logic. Russia is an original civilization. She is called not only to counter the West in order to safeguard its own path, but also to stand at the vanguard of the other peoples and countries of the Earth in order to defend their freedom as civilizations.

Criticism of the Roman-German civilization

Western civilization built its own system on the basis of the secularization of Western Christianity (Catholicism and Protestantism), bringing to the fore such values as individualism, egoism, competition, technical progress, consumption, and economic exploitation. The Roman-German civilization bases its right to global universality not upon spiritual greatness, but upon rough material force. Even the spirituality and strength of other peoples are evaluated by it only in terms of the Western notion of the supremacy of rationalism and technical progress.

The factor of space

There is no universal pattern of development. The plurality of landscapes on Earth produces a plurality of cultures, each one having its own cycles, internal criteria and logic. Geographical space has a huge (sometimes decisive) influence on peoples' culture and national history. Every people, as long as it develops within some given geographical environment, elaborates its own national, ethical, juridical, linguistic, ritual, economic, and political forms. The "place" where any people or state "development" happens predetermines to a great extent the path and sense of this "development" — up to the point when the two elements become one. It is impossible to separate history from spatial conditions, and the analysis of civilizations must proceed not only along the temporal axis ("before," "after," "developed" or "non-developed," and so on) but also along the spatial axis ("east," "west," "steppe," "mountains," and so on).

No single state or region has the right to claim to be the standard for all the rest. Every people has its own pattern of development, its own ages, and its own "rationality," and deserves to be understood and evaluated according to its own internal criteria.

The climate of Europe and the influence of its landscapes generated the particularity of European civilization, where the influences of the woods in northern Europe and of the coast in the Mediterranean prevail. Different landscapes generated different kinds of civilizations: the boundless steppes generated the nomad empires (from the Scythians to the Turks), the lower lands the Chinese one, the mountainous islands the Japanese one, and the union of the steppe and the woods the Russian-Eurasian one. The mark of a landscape lives in the entire history of each one of these civilizations, and cannot be either separated from them or suppressed.

State and nation

The first Russian Slavophiles in the nineteenth century (Khomyakov, Aksakov, Kirevsky) insisted upon the uniqueness and originality of Russian (Slavic and Orthodox) civilization. This must be defended, preserved and strengthened against the West, on the one hand, and against liberal modernism (which also proceeds from the West) on the other. The Slavophiles proclaimed the value of tradition, the greatness of ancient times, their love for the Russian past, and warned against the inevitable dangers of progress and about Russia's separation from many aspects of the Western pattern.

From this school the Eurasianists inherited the positions of the most recent Slavophiles and further developed their theses through a positive evaluation of Eastern influences.

The Muscovite Empire represents the highest development of Russian state-hood. In it, the national idea achieved a new status; after Moscow's refusal to rec-ognize the Florentine union of the Eastern and Western churches, which led to the arrest and proscription of the Metropolitan Isidore of Kiev who supported it, and the rapid decay of Byzantium, the Tsargrad Rus' inherited the mantle of the Orthodox empire.

Political platform

Wealth and prosperity, a strong state, an efficient economy, a powerful army and the development of production must be the instruments for the achievement of high ideals. The sense of the state and of the nation can be conferred only through the existence of a "leading idea." A political regime which supposes the establish-ment of a "leading idea" as a supreme value was called an "ideocracy" by the Eura-sianists, from the Greek *idea* and *kratos*, or power. Russia was always thought of by them as the Sacred Rus', as a power (*derzhava*) fulfilling its distinct historical mission. The Eurasianist worldview must also be the national idea of the coming Russia: its "leading idea."

The Eurasianist choice

Russia-Eurasia, being the expression of a "steppe and woods" empire of continental dimensions, requires her own pattern of leadership. This means, first of all, the ethics of collective responsibility, self-restraint, mutual aid, asceticism, willpower, and tenacity. Only such qualities can empower one to keep the wide and scarcely-populated lands of the steppe-woodland Eurasian zone under control. The ruling class of Eurasia was formed on the basis of collectivism, asceticism, warlike virtue, and rigid hierarchy.

Western democracy evolved under the particular conditions of ancient Athens and was shaped in the course of the centuries-old history of insular England. Such democracy mirrors the peculiar features of "local European development." Such democracy does not represent a universal standard. Imitating the forms of European "liberal democracy" is senseless, impossible and dangerous for Russia-Eurasia. The participation of the Russian people in political rule must be defined by a different term: *demotia*, from the Greek *demos*, or people. Such participation does not reject hierarchy and must not be formalized into party-parliamentary structures. *Demotia* supposes a system of land councils, district governments or national governments (in the case of smaller populations). It is developed on the basis of social self-government and on the "peasant" world. An example of *demotia* was the fact of the Church hierarchies being elected by the parishioners in Muscovite Rus'.

The Work of Lev Gumilev as a development of Eurasianist thinking

Lev Nikolayevich Gumilev (1912–1992), the son of the Russian poet Nikolai Gumilev and of the poetess Anna Akhmatova, was an ethnographer, historian and philosopher. He was profoundly influenced by the book of the Kalmyk Eurasianist, *Genghis Khan as an Army Leader* by E. Khara-Vadan, and by the works of Pyotr Savitsky. In its own works, Gumilev developed the fundamental Eurasianist theses. Towards the end of his life he called himself "the last of the Eurasianists."

Basic elements of Gumilev's theory

Gumilev's theory was passionarity (*passionarnost'*) as a development of Eurasianist idealism, the essence of which lies in the fact that every *ethnos*, as a natural formation, is subject to the influence of cosmic energies that cause the "passionarity effect," which is an active and intense way of living. In such conditions the *ethnos* undergoes a "genetic mutation," which leads to the birth of the "passionaries" — individuals of a special temper and talent. These become the creators of new ethnoses, cultures, and states. He drew scientific attention to the proto-history of the ancient, autochthonic peoples of the East and their colossal ethnic and cultural heritage. This was entirely absorbed by the great culture of the ancient epoch, but afterwards fell into oblivion (the Huns, Turks, Mongols, and so on). He also developed a Turkophile attitude in the theory of "ethnic complementarity."

An *ethnos* is generally any set of individuals or any "collective": a people, population, nation, tribe, or family clan, based on a common historical destiny. "Our Great-Russian ancestors," wrote Gumilev, "rather quickly and easily mixed with the Volga, Don and Obi Tatars and with the Buryats, who assimilated the Russian culture, during the fifteenth, sixteenth and seventeenth centuries. The same

Great-Russians mixed easily with the Yakuts, absorbing their identity and gradually coming into friendly contact with the Kazakhs and Kalmyks. Through intermar-
riage they peacefully coexisted with the Mongols in Central Asia, as the Mongols
themselves and the Turks, between the fourteenth and sixteenth centuries, were
fused with the Russians in Central Russia." Therefore the history of Muscovite
Rus' cannot be understood outside the framework of the ethnic contacts that took
place between the Russians and the Tatars, nor without that of the history of the
Eurasian continent.

The advent of neo-Eurasianism:
historical and social context

The crisis of the Soviet paradigm

In the mid-1980s, Soviet society began to lose its cohesiveness and its ability to
understand both itself and the outside world. Cracks began to appear in the Soviet
models of self-understanding. Society had lost its sense of orientation. Everybody
felt the need for change, but this was a confused feeling, since no one could predict
from which direction the change would come. At that time a rather unconvincing
divide began to appear between the "forces of progress" and the "forces of reaction"; the "reformers" and the "conservators of the past"; the "partisans of reform"
and the "enemies of reform."

Infatuation with the Western models

In that situation the term "reform" itself became a synonym for "liberal democracy." A hasty conclusion was inferred from the objective fact of the crisis of the
Soviet system which purported the superiority of the Western model and the necessity to copy it. On the theoretical level this was hardly self-evident, since the
"ideological map" offers a sharply more diverse array of choices than the primitive
dualism represented by the conflict of socialism versus capitalism, or of the Warsaw
Pact versus NATO. Yet it was precisely this primitive logic that prevailed: the "partisans of reform" became unconditional apologists for the West, whose structure
and logic they were ready to assimilate, while the "enemies of reform" proved to be
the inertia-bound preservers of the late Soviet system, whose structure and logic
became more and more obsolete. In such a condition of imbalance, the reformers/
pro-Westerners had on their side a potential for energy, novelty, expectations of

change, a creative drive, and new perspectives, while the "reactionaries" had nothing left but inertia, immobility, and appeals to the customary and familiar. It was in this psychological and aesthetic setting that liberal-democratic policy prevailed in Russia during the 1990s, although nobody had been allowed to make a clear and conscious choice.

The collapse of state unity

The result of these "reforms" was the collapse of the unity of the Soviet state and the beginning of the fall of Russia as the heir of the Soviet Union. The destruction of the Soviet system and its rationale was not accompanied by the creation of a new system and a new rationale developed in conformity with national and historical conditions. A peculiar attitude toward Russia and her national history began to prevail: the past, present and future of Russia began to be seen from the Western point of view, and to be evaluated as something estranged, transient, and alien (the "reformers" typically referred to Russia as "this country"). That was not the Russian view of the West so much as the Western view of Russia. It was no wonder that under such conditions the adoption of Western schemes even in the "reformers'" theory was invoked not in order to create and strengthen the structure of national state unity, but in order to destroy what remained of it. The destruction of the state was not a chance outcome of the "reforms"; it was in fact among their strategic aims.

The birth of an anti-Western (anti-liberal)
opposition in the post-Soviet environment

In the course of the "reforms" and their deepening, the inadequacy of merely reacting to the situation began to be clear to everyone. In that period (1989–90) the formation of a "national-patriotic opposition" began in which there was a confluence between a segment of the "Soviet conservatives" (those who were capable of a minimal level of reflection) and groups of "reformers" who were disappointed with the reforms or who had "become conscious of their anti-state direction," as well as with groups of representatives from the patriotic movements, which had already formed during *perestroika* and had tried to shape the sentiment of "state power" (*derzhava*) within a non-Communist (Orthodox-monarchic, nationalist, etc.) context. After a severe delay, and despite the complete absence of strategic, intellectual, and material support from outside, the conceptual model of post-Soviet patriotism began to vaguely take shape.

Neo-Eurasianism

Neo-Eurasianism arose in this framework as an ideological and political phenomenon, gradually becoming one of the main currents within the post-Soviet Russian patriotic self-consciousness.

Stages in the early development of neo-Eurasianist ideology

First stage (1985–90)

❋ Alexander Dugin gives seminars and lectures to various groups within the newborn conservative-patriotic movement. He offers criticism of the Soviet paradigm as lacking the spiritual and national qualitative element.

❋ In 1989 the first publications appear in the review *Sovetskaya literatura* (Soviet Literature). Dugin's books are published in Italy (*Continente Russia* [Continent Russia], 1989) and in Spain (*Rusia Misterio de Eurasia* [Russia, Mystery of Eurasia], 1990).

❋ In 1990 René Guénon's *The Crisis of the Modern World* is published in Russia with commentary by Dugin, as well as Dugin's *Puti Absoljuta* (The Paths of the Absolute), offering an exposition of the foundations of traditionalist philosophy.

❋ During these years Eurasianism displays "Right-wing conservative" features which are close to historical traditionalism, containing Orthodox-monarchic and "ethnic-*pochevennik*" (i.e., linked to ideas of soil and land) elements which are sharply critical of "Left-wing" ideologies.

Second stage (1991–93)

❋ A revision of the anti-Communism that was typical of the first stage of neo-Eurasianism begins. The Soviet period is reevaluated in the spirit of "National Bolshevism" and "Left-wing Eurasianism."

❋ The primary representatives of the "New Right" in Europe visit Moscow (Alain de Benoist, Robert Steuckers, Carlo Terracciano, Marco Battarra, Claudio Mutti, and others).

❋ Eurasianism becomes popular among the patriotic opposition and the intellectuals in Russia.

❋ On the basis of an affinity of terminology, Andrei Sakharov begins speaking about Eurasia, though only in a strictly geographic, instead of a political and geopolitical, sense (and without ever making use of Eurasianism in itself, as he was previously a convinced Atlanticist); a group of "democrats" tries to start a project of "democratic Eurasianism" (Gavriil Popov, Sergei Stankevic, and Lev Ponomaryov).

❋ Oleg Lobov, Oleg Soskovets, and Sergei Baburin also speak about their own forms of Eurasianism.

❋ In 1992–93 the first issue of *Elements: The Eurasianist Review* is published. Lectures on geopolitics and the foundations of Eurasianism are given in high schools and universities. Many translations, articles, and seminars appear.

Third stage (1994–98): theoretical development of neo-Eurasianist orthodoxy

❋ The publication of Dugin's primary works *Misterii Evrazii* (Mysteries of Eurasia, 1996), *Konspirologija* (Conspirology, 1994), *Osnovy Geopolitiki* (Foundations of Geopolitics, 1996), *Konservativnaja revoljutsija* (The Conservative Revolution, 1994), and *Tampliery proletariata* (Knight Templars of the Proletariat, 1997). The works of Trubetzkoy, Vernadsky, Alexeyev and Savitsky are issued by Agraf Editions during the period from 1995 until 1998.

❋ The Arctogaia Website is launched in 1996.

❋ Direct and indirect references to Eurasianism appear in the programs of the KPFR (Communist Party), LDPR (Liberal Democratic Party), and NDR (New Democratic Russia) — that is, on the Left, Right, and centre. A growing number of publications on Eurasianist themes appear, and many Eurasianist digests are issued.

✳ There begins to be criticism of Eurasianism from Russian nationalists, religious fundamentalists and orthodox Communists, as well as from the liberals.

✳ An academic, "weak" version of Eurasianism appears (from Profs. Alexander S. Panarin, Vitaly Y. Pashchenko, Fyodor Girenok and others) combined with elements of the Illuminist paradigm, which is rejected by Eurasianist orthodoxy. The latter then evolves towards more radically anti-Western, anti-liberal and anti-gobalist positions.

✳ Eurasianism attracts more and more followers in Kazakhstan. The President of Kazakhstan, Nursultan Nazarbayev, is himself an adherent of Eurasianist ideology. In this context, the opening of the Lev Gumilev University at Astana should be viewed as an event of crucial significance. In April 1994, Nazarbayev announces the idea of the "Eurasian Union." For the first time in the history of Eurasianism, a high-ranking politician voices support for its vision and offers concrete measures for its practical implementation. The groundbreaking nature of this event is analyzed and put into perspective in Dr. Dugin's essay, *The Eurasian Mission of Nursultan Nazarbayev* (2004).

Fourth stage (1998–2001)

✳ The gradual de-identification of neo-Eurasianism from its collateral political-cultural and party manifestations takes place; it instead turns in an autonomous direction (Arctogaia, New University, *Vtorzhenie* [Invasion]) outside the opposition and the extreme Left- and Right-wing movements.

✳ Apology of *staroobrjadchestvo* (Old Rite Orthodoxy).

✳ A shift to centrist political positions and support for Primakov as the new President. Dugin becomes an advisor to the Speaker of the Duma, Gennadiy N. Seleznyov.

✳ The publication of the Eurasianist booklet *Nash put'* (Our Path, 1998).

✳ The publication of *Evraziikoe Vtorzhenie* (Eurasianist Invasion) as a supplement to *Zavtra*. There is a growing distance from the opposition and a shift closer to the government's positions.

✳ Theoretical researches and expositions take place. *The Russian Thing* (*Russkaja vesch'*, 2001) is published. Further publications appear in the

Nezavisimaja Gazeta and *Moskovskij Novosti*, and the radio program *Finis Mundi* is broadcast on Radio 101. Additional radio broadcasts on geopolitical subjects and neo-Eurasianism occur on Radio *Svobodnaja Rossija* between 1998 and 2000.

Fifth stage (2001–2002)

⁕ The foundation of the Pan-Russian Political Social Movement Eurasia on "radical center" positions; declaration of full support to the President of the Russian Federation, Vladimir Putin on April 21, 2001.

⁕ The Chief Mufti of the Central Muslim Spiritual Directorate, Sheik Talgat Tadzhuddin, declares his support for the Eurasian Movement.

⁕ The periodical *Evraziizkoe obozrenie* (Eurasianist Review) begins publication.

⁕ Jewish neo-Eurasianism begins to appear (Avigdor Eskin, Avraam Shmulevich, and Vladimir Bukarsky).

⁕ The creation of the Website for the Eurasian Movement (www.eurasia.com. ru).

⁕ The conference, "Islamic Threat or Threat to Islam?" is held with the participation of Khozh-Ahmed Noukhayev, the Chechen theorist of "Islamic Eurasianism" ("Vedeno or Washington?", Moscow, 2001).

⁕ The publication of books by Erenzhen Khara-Davan and Yakov Bromberg (2002).

Sixth stage (2002–2003): establishment of the Eurasia political party

⁕ On May 30, 2002 at Saint Daniel's monastery in Moscow, a constituent (foundational) congress of the political party "Eurasia" is convened. Its program and charter is adopted and the party leader, Alexander Dugin, as well as the members of its political council, are elected.

⁕ The Eurasia political party disseminates Eurasianist ideas and publishes a series of monographs on the Eurasian agenda by Alexander Dugin: *The Program of the Political Party 'Eurasia'*, *Foundations of Eurasianism*, etc. An informational and analytical gateway on the Web is created: evrazia.info.

❋ Alexander Dugin publishes a number of articles on the Eurasian agenda in
   major Russian periodicals. Eurasianist writings begin appearing regularly in
   such major newspapers as *Rosssiyskaya Gazeta*, *Komsomolskaya Gazeta*, and
   Trud. Dugin participates in television programs of wide viewership, including *Vremya*, *Vremena* (Time and the Times, Channel 1), *Chto delat'?* (What
   to Do?, Channel Kultura), *Russkiy vzglyad* (Russian Outlook, Channel 3),
   Moment Istiny (Moment of Truth, Channel TVC), etc.

❋ The number of supporters of Eurasianism grows and new regional branches
   of the movement multiply.

Seventh stage (2003–2004): International Eurasianist Movement

❋ As the first Eurasianists had predicted, the format of a political party became an obstacle to the further development of Eurasianist ideology at the
   present time. The hopes that were invested in the party did not materialize.
   Eurasianism as a worldview has international appeal; most peoples of the
   Commonwealth of Independent States (CIS) countries, as well as multi-
   tudes abroad, share Eurasian values. Besides which the current political system in Russia has put up barriers between political parties and political convictions: most parliamentary parties are devoid of any convictions, while
   ideologically meaningful groups fall short of forming party structures. An
   account and analysis of the detrimental impact that was caused by the attempt to use the party format as a vehicle for Eurasianism led the Eurasianists to realize the necessity of abandoning the structure of a Russian political party in order to transform into a broader, international "Eurasianist
   Movement." In November 2003, the International Eurasian Movement
   Congress was held at the House of the Press in Moscow, and in December
   2003, the government officially recognized the Movement. From then on,
   the seventh stage in the development of Eurasianism began.

❋ The party cells of Eurasia begin to transform into branches of the Eurasian
   Movement. Many new groups and individual members start to join it. Organizational structures of the Eurasian Movement abroad come into existence in Kazakhstan, Belarus, Tajikistan, Kyrgyzstan, Ukraine, Azerbaijan,
   Armenia, Georgia, Bulgaria, Turkey, Lebanon, Italy, Germany, Belgium,

Great Britain, Spain, Serbia, Poland, Slovakia, Hungary, Canada, and the United States.

✳ The process of transformation from party cells into branches of the Movement in Russia and the creation of overseas organizations with their general headquarters in Moscow is accomplished by the end of 2004, and in December 2004 the party "Eurasia" was officially disbanded. From then on, the International Eurasian Movement, under the continuous leadership of Alexander Dugin, became the formational structure of Eurasianism. Many prominent political and religious leaders, as well as intellectuals and artists, from around the world become members of its Supreme Council.

✳ The following structures are created within the Eurasian Movement: the Eurasian Creative Union, the Eurasian Economic Club, the Analytical Department, the Publishing Department, the Department of Eurasian Education, and other structures.

✳ In his capacity as the leader of the International Eurasian Movement, in 2004 Alexander Dugin publishes the following monographs concerning the Eurasian agenda: *Philosophy of Politics*, *Project Eurasia*, *The Eurasian Mission of Nursultan Nazarbayev*, and *Philosophy of War*. A fundamental treatise by Dugin, *The Foundations of Geopolitics*, is published in Arabic in Beirut and in Serbian in Belgrade. In Italy, his *Conservative Revolution in Russia* is published. At the same time, Eurasianist work continues in both the Russian and international media.

✳ On April 2, 2004 in Astana, Alexander Dugin, along with President Nazarbayev, speaks at a conference dedicated to the tenth anniversary of the President's announcement of his "Eurasian Union" idea. On June 18, 2004, Dugin delivers a historic speech at the plenary meeting of the international conference, "Eurasian Integration: The Trends in Contemporary Development and the Challenges of Globalization," attended by the heads of state in the Eurasian Economic Community (EurAsEC). The Eurasian Movement organizes 32 actions of various sorts, including conferences, forums, symposiums, sessions of the Eurasian Economic Club, and congresses. Representatives of the Eurasian Movement take part in elections in Kazakhstan, Belarus and Ukraine as official monitors. 19 press conferences are organized. Dugin's public appearances include lectures on Eurasianism, geopolitics and political philosophy at 16 academies, universities, schools and other institutions of learning. Dugin successfully defends his doctoral dissertation, Transformation of Political Structures and Institutions within the Process of Modernization in Traditional Societies, at Rostov University. An honorary professorship is bestowed on Dr. Dugin by the Lev Gumilev University at Astana.

⁕　In December 2004, the Congress of Intellectual Eurasian Youth decides to create the Eurasianist Youth Union within the framework of the International Eurasianist Movement.

Basic philosophical positions of neo-Eurasianism

On the theoretical level, neo-Eurasianism consists of the revival of the classic principles of the movement in a qualitatively new historical phase, and of the transformation of these principles into the foundations of an ideological and political program, and a worldview. The heritage of the classical Eurasianists was accepted as the fundamental worldview for the ideological political struggle in the post-Soviet period, providing a spiritual-political platform of "total patriotism."

The neo-Eurasianists took the basic positions of classical Eurasianism and chose them as starting points for a platform, and as the main theoretical bases and foundations for their future development and practical application. In the theoretical field, neo-eurasists consciously developed the main principles of classical Eurasianism, taking into account the wide philosophical, cultural and political framework of the ideas of the twentieth century.

Each of the main positions of the classical Eurasianists has undergone a revival of its conceptual development.

Civilization concept

Criticism of Western bourgeois society from "Left-wing" (social) perspectives was superimposed onto the criticism of the same society from "Right-wing" (civilizational) perspectives. The Eurasianist idea about "rejecting the West" is thus reinforced by the rich weaponry of the "criticism of the West" that has been carried out by those in the West who disagree with the logic of its development (at least in recent centuries). The Eurasianist came only gradually — from the end of the 1980s to the mid-1990s — to this idea of fusing together the most different (and often politically contradictory) concepts that deny the "normative" character of Western civilization.

Criticism of the Roman-German civilization

Criticism of the Roman-German civilization was greatly stressed, being based on an analysis of the Anglo-Saxon world and of the US in particular. According to the spirit of the German Conservative Revolution and of the European "New Right," the "Western world" was differentiated into an Atlantic component (the US and England) and into a continental European component (properly speaking, a Roman-German component). Continental Europe is seen here as a neutral phenomenon, liable to be integrated — with some prerequisites — into the Eurasianist project.

The spatial factor

Neo-Eurasianism revolves around the idea of a complete revision of the history of philosophy according to geographical locations. We find the inspiration for this in the various models of the cyclical vision of history, from Danilevsky to Spengler, and from Toynbee to Gumilev.

Such a principle finds its most potent expression in traditionalist philosophy, which rejects theories of "evolution" and "progress," and founds this denial upon detailed metaphysical calculations, hence the traditional theory of "cosmic cycles," of the "multiple states of Being," of "sacred geography," and so on. The basic principles of the theory of cycles are expounded in detail in the works of René Guénon, as well as in those of other thinkers in this school of thought such as Gaston Georgel, Titus Burckhardt, Mircea Eliade, and Henry Corbin). A full rehabilitation has been given to the concept of "traditional society," namely those that either knew no history at all, or those which understand it according to their rites and myths of the "eternal return." The history of Russia is seen not simply as one of many local developments, but as the vanguard of the spatial system (East) that is opposed to the "temporal" one (West).

State and nation

Dialectics of national history

This leads Eurasianism to its final, "dogmatic" formulation, which includes the historiosophic paradigm of National Bolshevism (Nikolai Ustrialov) and its interpretation (Mikhail Agursky). The pattern is as follows:

❋ the Kiev period as the advent of the forthcoming national mission (from the ninth through the thirteenth centuries);

❋ the Mongolian-Tatar invasion as an obstacle to the levelling European trends; the geopolitical and administrative function of the Horde is handed over to the Russians; the division of the Russians between western and eastern Russians; differentiation occurs among various cultural kinds; the Great-Russians are formed on the basis of the "eastern Russians" under the Horde's control (from the thirteenth through the fifteenth centuries);

❋ the Muscovite Empire as the climax of the national-religious mission of Rus', the Third Rome (from the fifteenth to the end of the seventeenth century);

❋ the Roman-German yoke (the Romanovs); the collapse of national unity; separation between a pro-Western elite and the popular masses (from the end of the seventeenth to the beginning of the twentieth century);

❋ the Soviet period; revenge of the popular masses; the age of "Soviet messianism"; the re-establishment of the basic parameters of the main Muscovite line (the twentieth century);

❋ the phase of troubles that must end with a new Eurasianist push (the end of the twentieth century and the beginning of the twenty-first century).

Political platform

Neo-Eurasianism utilizes the methodology of Vilfredo Pareto's school, moves within the logic of the rehabilitation of the notion of organic hierarchy, picks up some Nietzschean motives, and develops the doctrine of the ontology of power, or of the Christian Orthodox concept of power as katechon. The idea of an elite leads us to the themes of the European traditionalists, who authored studies of the caste system in ancient society and of their ontology and sociology, including Guénon, Julius Evola, Georges Dumézil, and Louis Dumont. Gumilev's theory of "passionarity" also lies at the roots of the concept of the "new Eurasianist elite."

The thesis of *demotia*

The thesis of *demotia* is the continuation of the political theories of "organic democracy" that were developed by Jean-Jacques Rousseau, Carl Schmitt, Julien Freund, Alain de Benoist, and Arthur Moeller van den Bruck. The Eurasianist concept of "democracy" (*demotia*) is defined as the "participation of the people in its own destiny."

The thesis of "ideocracy"

The thesis of "ideocracy" lays a foundation for a call to the ideas of "conservative revolution" and the "Third Way," in the light of the experience of the Soviet, Israeli, and Islamic ideocracies, and analyzes the reasons for their historical failure. Critical reflection upon the qualitative content of the twentieth century ideocracy leads to a consistent criticism of the Soviet period (particularly the supremacy of quantitative concepts and secular theories, and the disproportionate given to the classist viewpoint).

The following elements contribute to the development of the ideas of the classical Eurasianists:

✳ **The philosophy of traditionalism** (Guénon, Evola, Burckhardt, and Corbin), which includes the idea of the radical decay of the "modern world," as well as the profound teachings of the Tradition. It also gives us the global concept of the "modern world" (negative category) as the antithesis of the "world of Tradition" (positive category) and accords criticism of Western civilization a basic metaphysical character, defining the eschatological, critical, and fatal content of the fundamental (intellectual, technological, political and economic) processes that have their origin in the West. The intuitions of the Russian conservatives, from the Slavophiles to the classical Eurasianists, are thereby completed by being provided with a fundamental theoretical base. (See Alexander Dugin, *Absoljutnaja Rodina* (The Absolute Homeland, Moscow 1999); *Konets Sveta* (The End of the World, Moscow 1997); and *Julius Evola et le conservatisme russe* (Julius Evola and Russian Conservatism, Rome 1997).

✳ **The investigation into the origins of sacredness** (Mircea Eliade, C. G. Jung, and Claude Lévi-Strauss) and representations of archaic consciousness as the manifestation of the paradigmatic complex which lies at the roots of culture. This is accompanied by the tracing of multifaceted human thinking and of culture into ancient psychic layers, where we find that fragments of archaic initiatic rites, myths, and primordial sacral complexes are concentrated. Likewise required is the interpretation of the contents of rational culture through the lens of ancient, pre-rational beliefs (see Alexander Dugin, *Evoljutsija paradigmal'nyh osnovanij nauki* (The Evolution of the Paradigmatic Foundations of Science, Moscow 2002).

✳ **The search for the symbolic paradigms of the space-time matrix,** which lies at the roots of rites, languages and symbols (see the work of Herman Wirth and other paleo-epigraphic investigations). This attempt to provide a foundation for the evidence found in the linguistic (Svityc-Illic), epigraphic (runology), mythological, folkloric, and ritual record, as well as in various monuments, allows us to rebuild an original map of the "sacred concept of the world" common to all the ancient Eurasian peoples, and demonstrates the existence of common roots (see Alexander Dugin's *Giperborejskaja Teorija* (Hyperborean Theory, Moscow 1993).

✳ **A reassessment of the development of geopolitical ideas in the West** (Sir Halford Mackinder, Karl Haushofer, Jordi von Lochhausen, Nicholas J. Spykman, Zbigniew Brzezinski, Jean Thiriart, and others). Since Mackinder's epoch, geopolitical science has developed significantly. The role of geopolitical constants in the history of the twentieth century appeared so clearly as to make geopolitics an autonomous discipline. Within the geopolitical framework, the concepts of Eurasianism and of Eurasia acquired a new, wider meaning. From some time thereafter, Eurasianism, in a geopolitical sense, began to indicate the continental configuration of a strategic (either existing or potential) bloc, centered on Russia or its enlarged base, and which was viewed as being opposed (either actively or passively) to the strategic initiatives of the opposed geopolitical pole: "Atlanticism."[2] During the mid-twentieth century, the United States came to replace Britain as the leader of this bloc. The philosophy and the political ideas contained in the Russian classics of Eurasianism have, in this situation, proven to be the most consequent and powerful expression (fulfilment) of Eurasianism in its strategic and geopolitical meaning. Thanks to the development of geopolitical research (see Alexander Dugin, *Osnovye geopolitiki* [Foundations of geopolitics, Moscow 1997]), neo-Eurasianism has become a methodologically evolved phenomenon. Especially remarkable is the meaning of the Land/ Sea duality (according to Carl Schmitt), which makes possible the use of this duality to understand an entire range of phenomena, from the history of religions to economics.

✳   **The search for a global alternative to mondialism** (globalism)[3] as an ultramodern phenomenon, which summarizes everything that is considered by both Eurasianism and neo-Eurasianism as being negative. Eurasianism in its wider meaning thus becomes the conceptual platform of anti-globalism, or of an alternative globalism. "Eurasianism" unites in itself all contemporary

---

2   Atlanticism is a geopolitical term denoting the Western sector of world civilization from the historical and geographical point of view; the member states of NATO from the military-strategic point of view (primarily the US); the unified information network created by the Western media empires from the cultural point of view; and the "market system" from the social point of view, which is claimed to be absolute and which denies all other forms for the organization of economic life. The Atlanticists are the strategists of the West and their conscious supporters in other parts of the world. They aim at putting the entire world under their control and seek to impose the social, economic and cultural attributes of Western civilization upon the rest of mankind. The Atlanticists are the builders of the "New World Order" — an unprecedented global system that benefits an absolute minority of the planet's population, the so-called "golden billion."

3   Globalism is the process of building the "New World Order," at the center of which stands the political-financial oligarchs of the West. The victims of this process are the sovereign states, national cultures, religious doctrines, economic traditions, efforts toward social justice, and the environment itself — every variety of spiritual, intellectual and material life on the planet. The term "globalism" in its usual political meaning denotes simply "unipolar globalism": i.e., not the fusion of different cultures, sociopolitical, and economic systems into something new — as this would be "multipolar globalism" or "Eurasianist globalism." It is the imposition of Western methods upon all of mankind.

trends that deny globalism any objective (let alone positive) content; it offers the anti-globalist intuition a new character of doctrinal understanding.

✳ **The assimilation of the social criticism of the "New Left" into a "conservative Right-wing interpretation,"** which refers to the heritage of Michel Foucault, Gilles Deleuze, Antonin Artaud, and Guy Debord. This also means the assimilation of the critical thinking of those who oppose the bourgeois Western system from the perspectives of anarchism, neo-Marxism, and so on. This conceptual pole represents a new stage of development in the "Left-wing" (National Bolshevik) tendencies which also existed among the first Eurasianists (Pyotr Suvchinsky, Lev Karsavin, Sergei Efron), and also provides a means for reaching a mutual understanding with the "Left" wing of anti-globalism.

✳ **"Third way" economics and the "autarchy of Great Spaces."** The application of heterodox economic models to the post-Soviet Russian reality, including the application of Friedrich List's theory of the "custom unions" and the actualization of the theories of Silvio Gesell, Joseph Schumpeter, and François Perroux, as well as a new Eurasianist interpretation of John Maynard Keynes.

The Common Home of Eurasia

International Eurasian Movement Program

Eurasian cultural dialogue: the basis of human history

Continent Eurasia is the cradle of human culture and civilization.

The Eurasian continent gave birth to different social, spiritual and political forms that together constitute the primary content of human history. Eurasia is dipolar. It consists of Europe and Asia, West and East. Human history is a constant dialogue and a dialectic exchange of energy, values, technology, ideas and other things that have been moving between these two poles for more than a thousand years.

East and West supplement each other.

Many nations and civilizations have crossed Eurasia from West to East and back. The ancestors of modern Europeans far ancestors moved across Asian deserts in hordes at the same time that the civilizations of China, India, and Persia flourished, having attained advanced philosophy, technology, and high standards of living. Each culture has its own historical timing, different from any other, and set to its own pace and mode of existence.

What we here and now call "savage" might be called "progress" tomorrow, and/or somewhere else. What we consider an absolute truism here and now might be considered merely a local and irrelevant cult in some other time or place. We should never worship the "here and now." The state of the world and its values are constantly changing. We must always check our judgments against the great scale of time and space.

Eurasia is a worthy scale by which to measure worthy notions. We must learn how think in a Eurasian fashion, and then we will be able to easily comprehend the nature of East and West, progress and Tradition, steadiness and flexibility, and loyalty both to the past and the future.

Globalization: a challenge to the nations and civilizations of the Eurasian continent

Today, in the era of globalization, a Eurasian dialogue between East and West is more important than ever before. Globalization comes from West but increasingly influences the East. This process is very complex and contradictory; it constantly raises new questions, sometimes quite dramatic and tense ones. The impact on Eurasia has been particularly acute. As a major stage for the process of globalization, it experiences it with great hardship since the continent is crossed by the major fault-lines and borders of the great cultures and civilizations.

Today as never before we need to comprehend the course, logic, and path of the process of history. Every day we need to make decisions that will affect future generations. It has become obvious that no single nation, confession, social class and or even civilization can solve these problems on its own. We increasingly have to listen to one other: Europe and Asia, Christians and Muslims, White and Black peoples, citizens of modern democratic states and places where traditional society survives. The key is to understand one another other correctly, avoid hasty conclusions, and acquire the true spirit of tolerance an respect toward those with different value systems, habits, and norms.

The Eurasian Movement is a venue for equitable, multilateral dialogue for sovereign subjects

In order to promote an intensive dialogue of cultures, civilizations, confessions, states, social groups both large and small, and ethnicities of the European continent in this new historical age, we declare the creation of the International Eurasian Movement.

Our movement has no preconceived notions, judgments, decisions or formulas to impose on anyone. We have many more questions than answers ahead. The true path can be reached only in the course of an open, consistent dialogue among all the major forces on our continent, from Tokyo to the Azores.

We call on those who feel a sense of responsibility for Eurasia and who are concerned with sustaining the spiritual essence of human life, discovering paths of historical development, values, and ideas, to come together and build a vision for the future. We must join our efforts in drawing an attainable map for the peoples of Eurasia for the new millennium.

We are deeply convinced that our common goal is to save the distinctive nature of nations, cultures, confessions, languages, values, and and philosophical systems that, as a whole, form the "blossoming variety" (Konstantin Leontiev) of our continent. Rapprochement and dialogue between countries and peoples should be achieved, but not at the price of losing our identities. We insist that maintaining one's identity is the highest value, which no one has the right to encroach upon. The participants in the dialogue of cultures and civilizations should be sovereign and free. Only such a dialogue can be just and meaningful.

We are strongly against globalization as a form of ideological, economic, political, and value-based imperialism. No one has the right to impose one's own private "truth," value system, and sociopolitical model by force or ruse upon the great nations of the Eurasian continent. Knowledge of Eurasian cultures allows us to realize how diverse our perceptions are of so many concepts. Even such notions as the individual, freedom, life", authority, law, justice, society, politics, and so on vary greatly in different cultural, linguistic, ethnic, and religious contexts. We ought to note all this in our multilateral Eurasian dialogue: so long as our diligent and responsible concern for "the others," "the ones who are different" is genuine, our future will be one of success, peace, and prosperity.

The nations of Eurasia must be free and independent.

West and East, every confession, ethnicity and culture have their own truths. We have all the reason to share our truth with others, but we must never impose it by force.

Against "Babylon blending" and the "new xenophobia"

Advances in science and technology have brought Eurasians closer to one another. However, at the same time ever sharper cultural, linguistic, and religious divisions and hurdles have come to the surface. New threats have been revealed: the "clash between civilizations," the new wave of terrorism, the outbreaks of interethnic and regional conflicts and wars. How can we make globalization compatible with the preservation of each national character and identity? How do we protect the continental rapprochement of peoples from turning into a global Babylon? How do we avoid a new wave of xenophobia and international strife? Our Movement is called to deal with these extremely complicated problems.

Eurasia as motherland

The Eurasian continent is not small and it is not big — it is sufficient. It is less than the whole planet but much more than any single national, cultural, or confessional region. Our challenge is to have all the peoples working for prosperity and peace all over the continent, erecting and maintaining our common Eurasian home. We aim high. Only the strong can succeed on this path. But our ancestors bequeathed us something great and vast: fountains of thought and noble spirit, the legacies of great empires and abundant economic strength, treasures of moral guidance and inspiration, a spectrum of varieties of possible social systems, and the riches of a thousand mother tongues.

Eurasia is a great foundation for the future, one cultivated by our ancestors over the course of millennia. Eurasia is our mother and our land. Entrusted to us, she is faithful to us. She empowers us, but she needs our protection and care. If we love and respect her, we will be rewarded with great riches.

The International Eurasian Movement can be seen as the eternal movement in the Tree of Life, from its roots to its crown and back again. The Movement is our hearts' pulse, and the pulse of our history. It will never cease so long as we live, breathe and act.

The Eurasian Idea

What is Eurasianism today?
What forms the concept of Eurasia?
Seven meanings of the word Eurasianism.
Evolution of the Eurasian idea.

Changes in the original meaning of Eurasianism

Various terms lose their original meaning though daily use over the course of many years. Such fundamental notions as socialism, capitalism, democracy, and fascism have changed profoundly. In fact, they have become banal.

The terms "Eurasianism" and "Eurasia" also contain some uncertainties because they are new, and belong to a new political language and intellectual context that is only coming into being today.

The Eurasian Idea mirrors a very active dynamic process. Its meaning has become clearer throughout the course of history but needs to be further developed.

Eurasianism as a philosophical struggle

The Eurasian Idea represents a fundamental revision of the political, ideological, ethnic, and religious history of mankind. It offers a new system of classification and categories that overcome standard clichés. The Eurasian theory has gone through two stages: a formational period of classical Eurasianism at the beginning of the twentieth century that was carried out by Russian émigré intellectuals (Trubetzkoy, Savitsky, Alexeyev, Suvchinsky, Ilin, Bromberg, Khara-Davan, etc.), and which was followed by the historical works of Lev Gumilev and, finally, by the formation of neo-Eurasianism from the second half of 1980s to the present.

Towards neo-Eurasianism

Classical Eurasian theory undoubtedly belongs to the past and can be correctly classified within the framework of the ideologies of the twentieth century. The time of classical Eurasianism may have passed, but neo-Eurasianism has become its second birth, with a new sense, scale, and meaning. When the Eurasian Idea arose from its ashes, it was less visible, but has since revealed its hidden potential.

Through neo-Eurasianism, the entire Eurasian theory has gained a new dimension. Today we cannot ignore the successes of neo-Eurasianism and we must try to comprehend it in its modern context. Furthermore, we will describe the various aspects of this notion.

Eurasianism as a Global Trend

Globalization as the vector of modern history

In the broad sense, the Eurasian Idea and even Eurasia as concept do not strictly correspond to the geographical boundaries of the Eurasian continent. The Eurasian Idea is a global-scale strategy that acknowledges the reality of globalization and the end of the "nation-states" (*État-nations*), but at the same time offers a different scenario for globalization which entails neither a unipolar world order nor universal world government. Instead, it suggests several global zones (poles). The Eurasian Idea is an alternative or multipolar version of globalization. Globalization is currently the major fundamental world process that is deciding the vector of modern history.

Paradigm of globalization, paradigm of Atlanticism

Today's nation-state is being transformed into a global state; we are facing the formation of planetary-wide governmental systems within a single administrative-economic system. It is wrong to believe that all nations, social classes, and economic models might suddenly begin cooperating on the basis of this new, planet-wide logic. Globalization is a one-dimensional, one-vector phenomenon that tries to universalize the Western (essentially Anglo-Saxon and American) point of view concerning how to best manage human history. It is the unification of different sociopolitical, ethnic, religious, and national structures into one system, a process that very often is connected to oppression and violence. It is a Western European historical trend that has reached its peak through the domination of the United States of America.

Globalization is the imposition of the Atlantic paradigm. The proponents of globalization, however, try to avoid admitting this at all costs. They argue that when there are no more alternatives to Atlanticism, it will stop being Atlanticism. The American political philosopher Francis Fukuyama writes about the "end of history," which actually means the end of geopolitical history and the conflict between Atlanticism and Eurasianism. This means a new architecture for a new world system that contains no opposition and only one pole — the pole of Atlanticism. We may also refer to this as the New World Order. The former model of opposition between two poles (East-West or North-South) is transformed into a model of the center versus the outskirts, in which the center is the West, or the "rich North," while the Global South is reduced to the outskirts). This variant of the world's architecture is completely at odds with the concept of Eurasianism.

There is an alternative to unipolar globalization

Today the New World Order is nothing more than a project, plan, or trend. It is very serious, but it is not fatal. Adherents of globalization deny having any particular plan for future, but today we are experiencing a large-scale phenomenon: contra-globalism, and the Eurasian Idea coordinates all the opponents of unipolar globalization in a constructive way. Moreover, it offers the competing idea of multipolar globalization (or alter-globalization).

Eurasianism as pluriversum

Eurasianism rejects the center-outskirt model of the world. Instead, the Eurasian Idea suggests that the planet consists of a constellation of autonomous living spaces that are partially open to each other. These areas are not nation-states, but rather a coalition of states, reorganized into continental federations or "democratic empires" with a large degree of domestic self-government. Each of these areas is multipolar, encompassing a complicated system of ethnic, cultural, religious, and administrative factors.

In this global sense, Eurasianism is open to everyone, regardless of one's place of birth, residence, nationality, or citizenship. Eurasianism provides an opportunity to choose a future that is different from the clichés of Atlanticism and its idea of a single value system for all of mankind. Eurasianism does not merely seek to revive the past or to preserve the current status quo, but strives for the future, acknowledging that the world's current structure needs radical change, and that nation-states and industrial society have exhausted all their resources. The Eurasian Idea does not advocate for the creation of a world government on the basis of liberal-democratic values as the one and only path for mankind. In its most basic sense, Eurasianism in the twenty-first century is defined as the adherence to alter-globalization, which is synonymous with the acknowledgment of a multipolar world.

Atlanticism is not universal

Eurasianism absolutely rejects the supposed universalism of Atlanticism and Americanism. The pattern of Western Europe and America has many attractive features that can be adopted and praised, but, as a whole, it is merely a cultural system that has a right to exist in its own historical and geographical context, but only alongside other civilizations and cultural systems.

The Eurasian Idea protects not only value systems that are anti-Atlanticist in nature, but also the diversity of value structures. It is a kind of pluriversum that provides living space for everyone, including the United States and Atlanticism, along with other civilizations, because Eurasianism also defends the civilizations of Africa, both American continents, and the Pacific area that runs parallel to the Eurasian Motherland.

The Eurasian Idea promotes a global revolutionary idea

The Eurasian Idea is a revolutionary concept on a global scale that is called upon to act as a new platform for mutual understanding and cooperation for a large conglomerate of different powers: states, nations, cultures, and religions that reject the Atlanticist version of globalization.

If we analyze the declarations and statements of various politicians, philosophers, and intellectuals, we will see that the majority of them are adherents, albeit sometimes unconsciously, of the Eurasian Idea.

If we consider all those who disagree with the postulation that we are at the "end of history," our spirits will rise, and our belief in the failure of the American conception of strategic security for the twenty-first century, which is dependent on creating and maintaining a unipolar model of the world, will appear much more realistic.

Eurasianism is the sum of the natural, artificial, objective, and subjective obstacles along the path to unipolar globalization; it offers a constructive, positive opposition to globalism instead of simple negation.

These obstacles remain uncoordinated for the time being, however, and the proponents of Atlanticism are able to easily deal with them. And yet, if these obstacles can somehow be integrated into a unified force, the likelihood of their victory will become much more probable.

Eurasianism as the Old World

The more specific and narrow meaning of the term Eurasianism pertains to what is traditionally called "the Old World." The notion of the Old World, which is typically used in reference to Europe, can be considered in a much wider context. It is a multi-civilizational superspace inhabited by nations, states, cultures, ethnicities, and religions that are connected to each other historically and geographically by dialectic destiny. The Old World is an organic product of human history.

The Old World is often opposed to the New World, and the American continent which, after having been discovered by Europeans, was transformed by them into a platform for an artificial civilization where European projects of modernism reached their fulfillment. It was constructed based upon man-made ideologies as a civilization of purified modernism.

The United States was the successful creature of the "perfect society," inspired by ideas proposed by intellectuals from England, Ireland, and France, while the countries of South and Central America remained colonies of the Old World. Germany and Eastern Europe were less influenced by this idea of a "perfect society."

Speaking in the terms of Oswald Spengler, the dualism between the Old and New World can be understood in terms of opposites: culture-civilization, organic-artificial, and historical-technical.

The New World as Messiah

As a historical product the evolution of Western Europe, very early on the New World realized its "messianic" destiny in which the liberal-democratic ideals of the Enlightenment were combined with the eschatological ideas of radical Protestant sects. This was called Manifest Destiny, and became the symbol of a new belief for generations of Americans. According to this theory, American civilization had overtaken all the cultures and civilizations of the Old World and the adoption of its universalist forms had now become obligatory for all the nations on the planet.

Over time, this theory came into direct collision not only with the cultures of the East and Asia, but also with Europe, which seemed to the Americans to be archaic, full of prejudice and antiquated traditions.

Eventually, the New World turned away from the heritage of the Old World. After the Second World War, the New World became the indisputable leader of Europe itself, setting the criteria by which its nations were to be evaluated. This inspired a corresponding wave of American dominance and at the same time the beginning of a movement that seeks geopolitical liberation from the strategic and economic domination of the brutal, transoceanic "elder Brother."

Integration of the Eurasian continent

In the twentieth century, the peoples of Europe became aware of their common identity and began to move, step by step, towards the integration of all Europe's nations into a common union which would be able to guarantee full sovereignty, security, and freedom for itself and all its members.

The creation of the European Union was crucial in helping Europe to restore its status as a world power alongside the United States. This was the response of the Old World to the intensive challenge offered by the New World.

If we consider the alliance of the US and Western Europe as the Atlantic vector of European development, the idea of European integration under the aegis of the continental countries (Germany and France) can be called European Eurasianism. This becomes more and more obvious if we take into consideration the idea of a Europe stretching from the Atlantic Ocean to the Urals (Charles de Gaulle's conception) or even to Vladivostok. In other words, the integration of the Old World should include the vast territory of the Russian Federation.

Thus, Eurasianism in this context may be defined as a project for the strategic, geopolitical, and economic integration of the northern region of the Eurasian continent, which is the cradle of European history and the matrix of the European peoples.

Along with Turkey, Russia, just as the ancestors of many Europeans, is historically connected to the Turkic, Mongolian, and Caucasus peoples. Russia offers the integration of Europe a Eurasian dimension in both the symbolic and geographical senses, in terms of the identification of Eurasianism with continentalism.

During the last few centuries, the revolutionary factions of Europe's elites have proposed the idea of European integration. In ancient times, similar attempts were made by Alexander the Great, who attempted to integrate the Eurasian continent, and Genghis Khan, who was the founder of history's largest empire.

Eurasia as three great living spaces, integrated across the meridian.

Three Eurasian belts (meridian zones)

The horizontal vector of integration is followed by a vertical vector.

Eurasian plans for the future presume the division of the planet into four vertical geographical belts, or meridian zones, from North to South.

Both American continents will form one common space oriented toward and controlled by the US within the framework of the Monroe Doctrine. This is the Atlantic meridian zone.

※   Additionally, three others are planned. They are the following:

※   Euro-Africa, with the European Union as its center;

※   the Russian-Central Asian zone;

※   the Pacific zone.

Within these zones, the regional division of labor and the creation of developmental areas and corridors of growth will take place.

Each of these belts (meridian zones) counterbalances each other, and all of them together counterbalance the Atlantic meridian zone. In the future, these belts might be the foundation upon which to build a multipolar model of the world: there will be more than two poles, but their number will be much less than the number of nation-states. The Eurasian model proposes that the number of poles must be four.

Great spaces

The meridian zones in the Eurasian project consist of several "Great Spaces" or "democratic empires." Each possesses relative freedom and independence but is strategically integrated into a corresponding meridian zone.

The Great Spaces correspond to the boundaries of civilizations and include several nation-states or unions of states.

The European Union and the Arab Great Space, which integrates North and Trans-Saharan Africa and the Middle East, forms Euro-Africa.

The Russian-Central Asian zone is formed by three Great Spaces that sometimes overlap one other. The first is the Russian Federation along with several countries of the CIS — the members of the Eurasian Union. The second is the Great Space of continental Islam (Turkey, Iran, Afghanistan, and Pakistan). The Asian countries of the CIS intersect with this zone.

The third Great Space is Hindustan, which is a self-sufficient civilizational zone.

The Pacific meridian zone is determined by a condominium of two Great Spaces, China and Japan, and also includes Indonesia, Malaysia, the Philippines, and Australia, the latter of which some researchers connect to the American meridian zone. This geopolitical region is very mosaic and can be differentiated by many criteria.

The American meridian zone consists of the American-Canadian, Central, and North American Great Spaces.

Importance of the fourth zone

The view of the world as being based upon meridian zones is accepted by most American geopoliticians who seek the creation of a New World Order and unipolar globalization. However, a stumbling bloc is the existence of the Russian-Central Asian meridian space: the presence or absence of this belt radically changes one's geopolitical picture of the world.

Atlanticist futurologists divide the world into the following three zones:

✳ the American pole, with the European Union as its close-range periphery (Euro-Africa as an exception);

✳ the Asian and Pacific regions as its long-range periphery;

✳ Russia and Central Asia are fractional, but without it as an independent meridian zone, our world is unipolar.

This last meridian zone counterbalances American pressure and provides the European and Pacific zones the ability to act as self-sufficient civilizational poles.

Real multipolar balance, freedom, and the independence of the meridian belts, Great Spaces, and the nation-states depends upon the successful creation of a fourth zone. Moreover, it is not enough to be one pole in a bipolar model of the world; the rapid progress of the United States can only be counterbalanced by the synergy of all three meridian zones.

The Eurasian Movement proposes that this four-zone super-project be realized on a geopolitical strategic level.

Eurasianism as Russian-Central Asian integration

Moscow-Tehran axis

The fourth meridian zone comprises the integration of the Russian-Central Asian meridian. The central issue of this process is the implementation of a Moscow-Tehran axis. The whole process of integration depends on the successful establishment of a strategic middle- and long-term partnership with Iran. The alliance of Iran and Russia's economic, military, and political potential will bolster the process of this zone's integration, which will make the development of this zone both irreversible and autonomous.

The Moscow-Tehran axis will be the basis for further integration. Both Moscow and Iran are self-sufficient powers, able to create their own organizational strategic model for the region.

Eurasian plan for Afghanistan and Pakistan

The integration vector with Iran is vitally important in order for Russia to gain access to warm-water ports, as well as for the political and religious reorganization of Central Asia (the Asian countries of the CIS, Afghanistan, and Pakistan). Close cooperation with Iran presumes the transformation of the Afghani-Pakistani area into a free Islamic confederation that is loyal to both Moscow and Tehran. The reason this is necessary is that the independent states of Afghanistan and Pakistan will continue to be a source of destabilization, threatening neighboring countries. Only the unification of the geopolitical efforts of all these nations will provide the ability to implement a new Central Asian federation and transform this complicated region into one of cooperation and prosperity.

Moscow-Delhi axis

Russian-Indian cooperation is the second-most important meridian axis in the integration of the Eurasian continent and the development of collective Eurasian security mechanisms. Moscow will play an important role in decreasing the tensions between Delhi and Islamabad over Kashmir. The Eurasian plan for India, sponsored by Moscow, entails the creation of a federation that will mirror the diversity of Indian society with its numerous ethnic and religious minorities, including Sikhs, Jains, Zoroastrians, Christians, and Muslims.

Moscow-Ankara

Our main regional partner in the integration process of Central Asia is Turkey. The Eurasian Idea is already becoming rather popular there today because of Western trends that have become interlaced with Eastern ones. Turkey acknowledges its civilizational differences with the European Union, and recognizes the importance of Eurasianism for its regional goals and interests, as well as in countering the threat of globalization and a further loss of its sovereignty.

It is vitally imperative for Turkey to establish a strategic partnership with the Russian Federation and Iran. Turkey will only be able to maintain its traditions within the framework of a multipolar world. Certain factions of Turkish society understand this situation, from politicians and socialists to the religious and military elites. Thus, the Moscow-Ankara axis can become a geopolitical reality despite a long period of mutual estrangement.

The Caucasus

The Caucasus is the most problematic region for Eurasian integration because its mosaic of cultures and ethnicities easily leads to tensions between peoples. This is one of the main weapons used by those who seek to put an end to processes of integration across the Eurasian continent. The Caucasus region is inhabited by peoples belonging to different states and civilizational areas. This region must be a polygon for testing different methods of cooperation between peoples, because what can succeed there can succeed across the Eurasian continent. The Eurasian solution to this problem lies not in the creation of ethnic-based states or in assigning one people strictly to one state, but in the development of a flexible federation on the basis of ethnic and cultural entities within the common strategic context of the meridian zone.

The goal of this plan is a half-axis system between Moscow and the Caucasian centers (Moscow-Baku, Moscow-Erevan, Moscow-Tbilisi, Moscow-Makhachkala,

Moscow-Grozny, etc.) and between the Caucasian centers and Russia's allies within the Eurasian project (Baku-Ankara, Erevan-Tehran, etc.).

The Eurasian plan for Central Asia

Central Asia must move towards integration into a united strategic and economic bloc with the Russian Federation within the framework of the Eurasian Union, which is the successor to the CIS. The main function of this specific area is the rapprochement of Russia with the countries of continental Islam (Iran, Pakistan, and Afghanistan).

From the very beginning, the Central Asian sector must have various vectors of integration. One such plan would make the Russian Federation its main partner due to similarities of culture, common economic and resource-related interests, as well as the need for a common strategic security alliance). An alternate plan is to place the accent on ethnic and religious similarities: the Turkic, Iranian, and Islamic worlds.

Eurasian integration of post-Soviet territories

Eurasian Union

A more specific meaning for Eurasianism, which is in part similar to the definitions given by the early intellectuals of Eurasianism, is connected with the process of the local integration of the post-Soviet territories.

Different forms of a similar integration can be seen throughout history, from the Huns and other nomadic empires (namely the Mongol, Turkic, and Indo-European) to the empire of Genghis Khan and his successors. More recent efforts at integration were led by the Romanov Empire of Russia and, later, the Soviet Union. Today, the Eurasian Union is continuing these traditions of integration using a unique ideological model that takes democratic procedures into consideration, respects the rights of its nations, and pays attention to the cultural, linguistic, and ethnic features of all members of the Union.

Eurasianism is the philosophy of the integration of the post-Soviet territory on a democratic, non-violent, and voluntary basis without the domination of any single religious or ethnic group.

Astana, Dushanbe, and Bishkek as the main force of integration

The various Asian republics of the CIS address the process of post-Soviet integration in different ways. The most active adherent to integration is Kazakhstan. President Nursultan Nazarbayev is a staunch supporter of the Eurasian Idea. Kyrgyzstan and Tajikistan likewise support the process of integration, although their support is less tangible in comparison with Kazakhstan.

Tashkent and Ashabad

Uzbekistan and especially Turkmenistan oppose the integration process in an effort to exploit their recently achieved national sovereignty for their own gain. However, very soon, due to the increasing rate of globalization, both states will face a dilemma: will they lose their sovereignty and melt into a unified, globalist world dominated by American liberal values, or will they preserve their cultural and religious identities in the context of the Eurasian Union? In our opinion, an unbiased comparison of these two options will lead to the adoption of the second one, which follows naturally for both countries because of their histories.

The Trans-Caucasian states

Armenia continues to gravitate towards the Eurasian Union and considers the Russian Federation to be an important supporter and conciliator that helps it to manage relations with its Muslim neighbors. It is notable that Tehran prefers to establish a partnership with the Armenians, who are ethnically close to them. This fact allows us to consider two half-axes — Moscow-Erevan and Erevan-Tehran — as necessary prerequisites for integration.

Baku remains neutral, but this situation will change drastically with the continued movement of Ankara towards Eurasianism, which will have immediate consequences for Azerbaijan. An analysis of Azerbaijani culture shows that this state is closer to the Russian Federation and the post-Soviet republics of the Caucasus and Central Asia than to religious Iran, and even to moderate Turkey.

Georgia is the key problem of the region. The mosaic character of the Georgian state has been the cause of serious problems during the construction of a new national state that is strongly rejected by its ethnic minorities: Abkhazia, South Ossetia, Adjara, and so on. Furthermore, the Georgian state does not have any strong partners in the region and is thus forced to seek a partnership with the United

States and NATO to counterbalance Russian influence. Georgia is a major threat and is capable of sabotaging the very process of Eurasian integration. The solution to this problem is to be found in the Orthodox culture of Georgia, with its Eurasian features and traditions.

Ukraine and Belarus: the Slavic countries of the CIS

It is enough to gain the support of Kazakhstan and Ukraine to succeed in the creation of the Eurasian Union. The Moscow-Astana-Kiev geopolitical triangle is a frame that will be able to guarantee the stability of the Eurasian Union, which is why negotiations with Kiev are urgent as never before. Russia and Ukraine have very much in common: cultural, linguistic, religious, and ethnic similarities. These aspects need to be highlighted because Russophobia and separation from Russia have been promoted in Ukraine since the beginning of its recent sovereignty.

Many countries of the EU can positively influence the Ukrainian government because they are interested in promoting political harmony in Eastern Europe. Cooperation between Moscow and Kiev will demonstrate the pan-European attitudes of both Slavic countries.

The above-mentioned factors also pertain to Belarus, where the intention to integrate is much more evident. However, the strategic and economic status of Belarus is less important to Moscow than those of Kiev and Astana. Moreover, the domination of a Moscow-Minsk axis will harm the prospects for integration with Ukraine and Kazakhstan. That is why integration with Belarus must proceed smoothly and without any sudden incidents, in tandem with other vectors of the Eurasian integration process.

Eurasianism as *Weltanschauung*

The last definition of Eurasianism characterizes a specific *Weltanschauung*: a political philosophy that combines tradition, modernity, and even elements of postmodernism. This philosophy has traditional society as its priority. It acknowledges the imperative of technical and social modernization without disregarding traditional culture, and strives for the adaptation of its ideological program towards a type of post-industrial and informational society called postmodernism.

Postmodernism removes the formal contradistinction between tradition and modernism. However, the Atlanticist brand of postmodernism views both tradition and modernism as being outdated and devoid of meaning. Eurasian postmodernism, on the contrary, promotes an alliance of tradition and modernism as a constructive, optimistic, and energetic impulse towards creation and growth.

Eurasian philosophy does not deny the realities that were dismissed by the Enlightenment: religion, ethnicity, empire, culture, and so on. At the same time, the best achievements of modernism should be widely adopted: among them technological and economic advances, social guarantees, and freedom of labor. Extremes meet each other, melting into a unifying harmonious and original theory that will inspire fresh thinking and new solutions to the eternal problems people have faced throughout history.

Eurasianism is an open philosophy

Eurasianism is an open, non-dogmatic philosophy that can be enriched with new content: religion, sociological and ethnological discoveries, geopolitics, economics, national geography, culture, strategic and political research, etc. Moreover, Eurasian philosophy offers original solutions in specific cultural and lingual contexts: Russian Eurasianism will not be the same as French, German, or Iranian versions. However, the main framework of the philosophy will remain invariable.

The principles of Eurasianism

The basic principles of Eurasianism are as follows:

- ✳ differentialism: a plurality of value systems versus the conventional and obligatory domination of a single ideology (American liberal democracy first and foremost);
- ✳ tradition versus the suppression of cultures, their dogmas, and the wisdom of traditional society ;
- ✳ the rights of nations versus the "golden billion" and the neocolonial hegemony of the "rich North";
- ✳ ethnicities as the primary value and the subjects of history versus the homogenization of peoples, which are to be imprisoned within artificial social constructions;
- ✳ social fairness and human solidarity versus exploitation and the humiliation of man by man.

Map of unipolar world

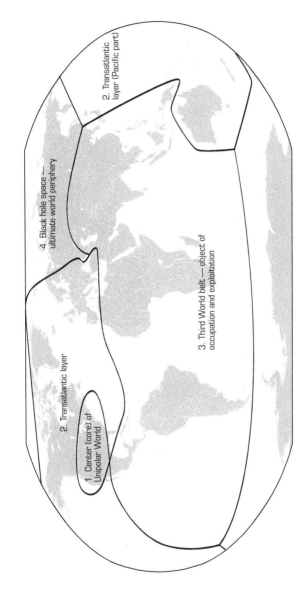

1. Center (core) of Unipolar World

2. Transatlantic layer

4. Black hole space — ultimate world periphery

2. Transatlantic layer (Pacific part)

3. Third World belt — object of occupation and exploitation

1. Central nucleus
2-3. Peripheral layers
4. Black hole land

Map of Russian-Eurasian reaction against unipolar globalization
— Counter-strategy

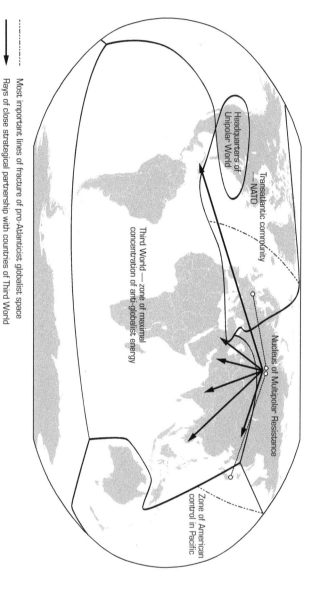

Headquarters of
Unipolar World

Transatlantic community
— NATO

Third World — zone of maximal
concentration of anti-globalist energy

Nucleus of Multipolar Resistance

Zone of American
control in Pacific

Most important lines of fracture of pro-Atlanticist globalist space

Rays of close strategical partnership with countries of Third World

Crucial axes of alliances of Eurasian geopolitics with "emerging
empires" — Great Europe and free Japan

Map of multi-polar world: Four zones — four poles

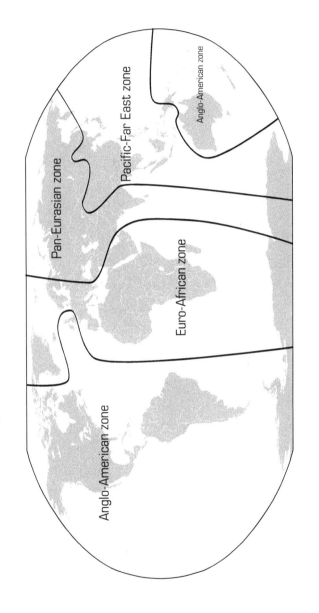

Pan-Eurasian zone

Pacific-Far East zone

Anglo-American zone

Anglo-American zone

Euro-African zone

2-d map of multi-polar world: Four zones — Large Spaces

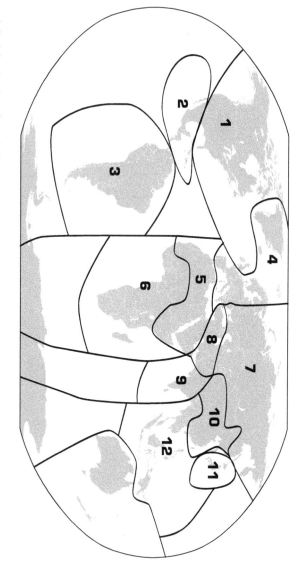

1. North American Large Space. 2. Central American Large Space. 3. South American Large Space. 4. European Large Space. 5. Arabo-Islamic Large Space. 6. Trans-Saharan Large Space. 7. Russian-Eurasian Large Space. 8. Islamic continental Large Space. 9. Hindu Large Space. 10. Chinese Large Space. 11. Japanese Large Space. 12. New Pacific Large Space.

The Eurasianist Vision I

The Basic Principles of the Eurasianist Doctrinal Platform

> According to to 71% of Russian citizens who were surveyed, Russia belongs to a unique — Eurasian or Orthodox — civilization, and therefore she does not follow the Western method of development. Only 13% consider Russia as a Western civilization.
>
> — From a survey by the Russian Public Opinion
> Research Centre, November 2–5, 2001

The breath of the epoch

Every historical epoch has its own peculiar "system of coordinates" — politically, ideologically, economically, and culturally.

For example, the nineteenth century in Russia was defined by the dispute between the "Slavophiles" and the "Pro-Westerners" (*zapadniki*). The twentieth century's watershed conflict took place between the "Reds" and the "Whites." The twenty-first century will be the century of opposition between the "Atlanticists" (the supporters of "unipolar globalism") and the "Eurasianists."

Against the establishment of the Atlanticist world order and globalisation stand the supporters of the multipolar world: the Eurasianists. The Eurasianists defend on principle the necessity to preserve the existence of every people on Earth, the blossoming variety of cultures and religious traditions, and the unquestionable right of the peoples to independently choose their own path of historical development. The Eurasianists greet the dialogue of cultures and value systems with enthusiasm, and they cherish the organic combination of devotion to traditions and creative cultural innovations.

The Eurasianists are not only the representatives of the peoples who live on the Eurasian continent. Being a Eurasianist is a conscious choice, which means combining the aspiration to preserve the traditional forms of life with the aspiration toward free and creative development, both social and personal.

In this way, Eurasianists are all free creative personalities who acknowledge the values of tradition. Among them are also representatives of those regions which objectively form the bases of Atlanticism.

Eurasianists and Atlanticists are opposed to each other in everything. They defend two different and mutually exclusive images of the world and its future. It is the opposition between Eurasianists and Atlanticists which defines the historical outline of the twenty-first century.

The Eurasianist vision of the future world

The Eurasianists consequently defend the principle of multipolarity, standing against the project of unipolar globalism that is being imposed by the Atlanticists.

According to the Eurasian vision of this new world, there will no longer be traditional states. Instead, there will be new, integrated civilizational structures ("Great Spaces"), united into "geo-economic belts" ("geo-economic zones").

According to the principle of multipolarity, the future of the world is imagined as an equal, benevolent form of relations and a partnership among all countries and peoples, organized — according to a principle of relation through proximity in terms of geography, culture, values, and civilization — into four geo-economic belts, each one consisting in its turn of some of these Great Spaces:

- ✳ the Euro-African belt, inclusive of three Great Spaces: the European Union, Islamic-Arab Africa, and sub-Saharan (Black) Africa;

- ✳ the Asian-Pacific belt, inclusive of Japan, the countries of Southeastern Asia, Indochina, Australia, and New Zealand;

- ✳ the Eurasian continental belt, which is inclusive of four Great Spaces: Russia and the countries of the Commonwealth of Independent States, the countries of continental Islam, India, and China;

- ✳ the American belt, which is inclusive of three Great Spaces: North America, Central America and South America.

Thanks to such an organization of the world, global conflicts, bloody localized wars, and other extreme forms of confrontation which threaten the very existence of mankind, would become less likely.

Russia and its partners in the Eurasian continental belt will establish harmonious relations not only with the neighboring belts (the Euro-African and Asia-Pacific), but also with its antipode: the American belt, which will also be called to play a constructive role in the Western hemisphere within the context of the multipolar order.

Such a vision of the future of mankind is the opposite of the globalists' plans, which are aimed at creating a unipolar, prepackaged New World Order under the control of the oligarchic structures of the West, which will ultimately lead to world government.

The Eurasianist vision of the evolution of the state

The Eurasianists consider the nation-state, in their present reality, as an obsolete form of organization of spaces and peoples which was typical of the historical period from the fifteenth to the twentieth centuries. In the place of nation-states, new political formations must arise, combining within themselves the strategic unification of the great continental spaces with the complex, multi-dimensional system of national, cultural, and economic autonomies. Some features of such an organization of spaces and peoples may be observed both in the ancient empires of the past (e.g., the empire of Alexander the Great, the Roman Empire, etc.) and in some of the newest political structures, such as the European Union and the CIS.

Contemporary states must choose from the following options:

✳ self-liquidation and integration into a single planetary space under American domination (Atlanticism, globalization);

✳ opposition to globalization while attempting to preserve their own administrative structures and formal sovereignty in spite of it;

✳ entering into supra-state formations of a regional nature (Great Spaces) on the basis of historical, civilizational, and strategic commonalities.

The third option is the Eurasianist one. From the point of view of a Eurasianist analysis, this is the only mode of development that is capable of preserving everything that is most valuable and original which contemporary states are called to safeguard in the face of globalization. The merely conservative aspiration to preserve the state at any cost is doomed to failure. The conscious desire of the political leaderships of many states to simply dissolve into the globalist project is viewed by the Eurasianists as the renunciation of those values whose preservation has always been the responsibility of the leaders of the nation-states toward their subjects.

The twenty-first century shall be the arena of the fateful decisions by the political elites when they choose between these three options. The struggle for the third option lies at the foundations of a new and broad international coalition of political forces that are in tune with the Eurasianist worldview.

The Eurasianists consider the Russian Federation and the CIS as the nucleus of a forthcoming autonomous political formation: the "Eurasian Union" ("core Eurasia"), as well as being one of the four basic geo-economic belts of the world (the Eurasian continental bloc).

At the same time, the Eurasianists strongly favor the development of a multi-dimensional system of autonomies.[1]

We view the principle of multi-dimensional autonomy as the optimal organizational structure for peoples, as well as ethnic and social-cultural groups in the Russian Federation, the European Union, the Eurasian continental belt and all the other Great Spaces and geo-economic belts (or zones).

All the territories of the new political-strategic Great Spaces must be placed under the direct management of a center of strategic government. Within the competence of the autonomy remain issues linked to the non-territorial aspects of the management of these zones.

---

1   Autonomy (which is derived from the ancient Greek *autonomos*, or self-government) is the form of the natural organization of a community, which is united by some kind of organic feature (national, religious, professional, familial, etc.). A distinctive feature of autonomy is that it offers the greatest amount of freedom to communities in those spheres that are not concerned with the strategic interests of the Great Spaces in which they exist. Autonomy is opposed to sovereignty — a feature of the organizations of peoples and spaces typical of the nation-states in their present form. In the case of sovereignty, we are dealing with the prioritization of the right to free and independent management of the territory that is under the purview of a community; autonomy supposes independence for communities in those issues pertaining to the organization of the collective life of peoples and regions, but not linked to the management of the territory.

The Eurasianist principle of the division of powers

The Eurasianist principle of political management proposes two different levels of government: local and strategic.

At the local level, the government is controlled through the autonomies — of course being composed of associations of different kinds, from those with millions of people to small collectivities consisting of only a few workers. This government will be absolutely unconstrained in its actions and will not be regulated by any higher authorities. The model for any type of autonomies will be freely chosen, stemming from tradition, inclination, and the direct democratic expression of the will of the organic communities within it, including all types of societies, groupings, and religious organizations.

The following will be placed under the management of the autonomies:

* civil and administrative issues;
* the social sphere;
* education and medical services;
* all spheres of economic activity.

In other words, everything will fall under the purview of the autonomies apart from the strategic branches and those issues concerning security and the territorial integrity of the Great Spaces.

The level of freedom for the citizenry, thanks to the organization of society according to the Eurasianist principle of autonomy, will be unprecedentedly high. Each individual will be given possibilities for self-realization and creative development never before seen in the history of mankind.

The issues of strategic security and those activities on the international level beyond the frame of a single continental space, such as macro-level economic issues, control over strategic resources, and communications, will be kept under the management of a single strategic center.[2]

---

2   A single strategic center is a conventional definition for all those instances when control is delegated to the strategic regional governments of the Great Spaces. It is a rigidly hierarchical structure, combining elements of the military, the judiciary and the administrative branches. It is the center for geopolitical planning and for the government of the Great Spaces.

The balance between the strategic and local levels of power will be strictly delimited. Any attempt to introduce the autonomy into the issues which fall under the purview of the single strategic center must be precluded. The reverse is also true.

In this way, the Eurasianist principles of government organically combine traditional and religious rights, and national and local traditions take into account all the riches of the sociopolitical regimes which formed in the course of the region's history. This system therefore offers a solid guarantee of stability, security and territorial integrity.

The Eurasianist vision of the economy

The Atlanticists' aim is to impose a single model of economic order on all peoples in the world, elevating the experience of the economic development of the Western part of world civilization in the nineteenth and twentieth centuries to the status of a universal standard.

In opposition to this, the Eurasianists are convinced that economic systems should be derived from the historical and cultural features of the development of peoples and societies they affect; consequently, in the economic sphere Eurasianists conform to the ideal of variety, a plurality of systems, the need for creative research, and free development.

Only those large-scale sectors of the economy that are linked to the need to ensure the security of an autonomy (the military-industrial complex, transportation, natural resources, energy, and communications) should be subject to rigid control. All the other sectors must freely and organically develop in accordance with the conditions and traditions of the concrete autonomies where such economic activity is taking place.

Eurasianism arrives at the conclusion that, in the field of economics, there is no ultimate truth — the recipes of liberalism[3] and Marxism[4] can only be partially applied, depending on the actual conditions of a society. In practice, the free market approach has to be combined with control over the strategic sectors of the economy. Redistribution of profits needs to be controlled according to the national and social aims of the society as a whole. In this way, Eurasianism conforms to the "third way"[5] model of economics.

The economics of Eurasianism must be built according to the following principles:

* the subordination of the economy to higher civilizational spiritual values;

* the principle of macro-economic integration and the division of labor on the scale of the Great Spaces (a customs union);

* the creation of a single financial, transportation, energy, productivity and informational system within the Eurasian space;

* the establishment of differentiating economic borders with neighboring Great Spaces and geo-economic zones;

* strategic control of the branches that form the basis of the economy by the center in tandem with maximal freedom of economic activity at the level of medium- and small-scale businesses;

* the organic combination of the forms of economic management (the market structure) with the social, national and cultural traditions of the regions through the lack of a uniform economic standard in medium and large enterprises.

---

3   Liberalism is an economic doctrine which maintains that only the absolute freedom of the market and the privatization of all elements of an economy can create the optimal conditions for economic growth. Liberalism is the dogmatic economic doctrine of the Atlanticists and the globalists.

4   Marxism is an economic doctrine which maintains that only by some social body exercising full control over the economic process, the logic of compulsory general planning, and the equal distribution of surplus productivity among all members of a society (collectivism) can lay the economic foundations for a just world. Marxism rejects the market and the concept of private property.

5   "Third way" economics is a set of economic theories which combine the market approach with the concept of the regulated economy on the basis of supra-economic criteria and principles.

The Eurasianist vision of finance

The single strategic center of the Eurasian Union must also consider the issue of control over monetary circulation as being strategically relevant. No single currency must pretend to the role of being the universal reserve currency for the entire world. It is necessary to create a proper Eurasian reserve currency, which will be the legal tender within those territories belonging to the Eurasian Union. No other currency shall be used within the Eurasian Union as a reserve currency.

On the other hand, the creation of local means of payment and exchange, being the legal tender within one or several of the neighboring autonomies, must be encouraged in every way. This measure prevents the accumulation of capital for speculative purposes and provides a stimulus to its circulation. Besides which it increases the size of investment into the real sector of the economy. Therefore, funds will be invested first of all where they can be productively employed.

In the Eurasianist project, the financial sphere is seen as an instrument of real production and exchange, directed towards the qualitative side of economic development. As opposed to the Atlanticist, globalist project, the financial sphere must have no autonomy (financialism)[6] whatsoever.

The regional vision of the multipolar world supposes different levels of currency:

* geo-economic currency (money and paper values, being the legal tender within a definite geo-economic zone, as the instrument of financial relations among the strategic centers of a set of Great Spaces);

* Great Space currency (money and paper values, being the legal tender within a specific Great Space — particularly within the Eurasian Union — as the instrument of financial relations among the autonomies);

* currency (different forms of equivalent exchange) at the level of the autonomies.

---

6   Financialism is the economic system of capitalism society in its post-industrial stage, being the logical result of the unlimited development of liberal principles in economics. Its distinctive feature is that the real sector of the economy becomes subordinated to virtual financial operations (stock markets, financial paper markets, portfolio investments, operations with international liabilities, futures transactions, speculative forecasting of financial trends, etc.). Financialism hinges upon monetarist policies, separating the monetary area (world reserve currencies and electronic money) from production.

In accordance with this scheme, issuing and financial credit institutions (banks), regional banks, banks of the Great Spaces, and banks of the autonomies (and their equivalents) must be organized.

The Eurasianist attitude toward religion

In devotion to the spiritual heritage of one's ancestors and in the meaningful religious life, the Eurasianists see a step toward an authentic renewal and harmonic social development.

The Atlanticists in principle refuse to see anything but the ephemeral, the temporary, and the present. For them there is essentially neither past nor future.

The philosophy of Eurasianism, on the contrary, combines a deep and sincere trust in the past with an open attitude toward the future. The Eurasianists accept fidelity to religious traditions as well as to free, creative research.

For the Eurasianists, spiritual development is the main priority of life, which cannot be replaced by amy economic or social benefits.

In the opinion of the Eurasianists, every local religious tradition or system of faith, even the most insignificant, is the patrimony of all mankind. The traditional religions of the peoples, which are connected to the various spiritual and cultural heritages of the world, deserve the utmost care and concern. The representative organizations of the traditional religions must be supported by the strategic centers. Schismatic groups, extremist religious associations, totalitarian sects, preachers of non-traditional religious doctrines and teachings, and any other forces that promote the destruction of traditional religions must be actively opposed.

The Eurasianist view of the national question

The Eurasianists believe that every people in the world, from those who founded great civilizations to the smaller ones, and which are carefully preserving their traditions, are an inestimable wealth. The assimilation of a people through external influences, the loss of a language or a traditional way of life, or the physical extinction of any of the peoples of the Earth is an irreparable loss for all mankind.

Eurasianists call the profusion of peoples, cultures, and traditions "blossoming variety," a sign of the healthy, harmonic development of human civilization.

The Great Russians, in this connection, represent a unique case of the fusion of three ethnical components — the Slavic, Turkish and Finno-Ugric — into one people, with an original tradition and a rich culture. The very fact of the rise of the Great Russians from the synthesis of three ethnical groups contains an integration potential of exceptional worth. For this same reason Russia became the core of the union of many different peoples and cultures into one single civilizational fusion on more than one occasion. The Eurasianists believe that Russia is destined to play the same role in the twenty-first century.

The Eurasianists are not isolationists, to the same extent that they are not supporters of assimilation at any cost. The life and destiny of peoples is an organic process which does not tolerate any artificial interference. Inter-ethnic and international issues must be decided according to their inner logic. Every people on Earth should have the freedom to independently make their own historical choices. Nobody has the right to force any people to give up its uniqueness by going into the "global melting pot," as the Atlanticists would have.

The rights of the peoples are no less significant to the Eurasianists than the rights of individuals.

Eurasia as a planet

Eurasianism is a worldview, a philosophy, a geopolitical project, an economic theory, a spiritual movement, and a nucleus around which to consolidate a broad spectrum of political forces. Eurasianism is free from dogmatism and from the blind submission to the authorities and ideologies of the past. Eurasianism is the ideal platform for the inhabitant of the New World, for whom disputes, wars, conflicts, and myths of the past hold no more than historical interest. Eurasianism as a principle is the new worldview for the new generations of the new millennium. Eurasianism draws its inspiration from various philosophical, political, and spiritual doctrines, which until now appeared irreconcilable and incompatible.

Together with this, Eurasianism has a definite set of basic founding ideas from which a Eurasianist cannot deviate under any circumstances. One of the main principles of Eurasianism is consistent, active, and widespread opposition to the unipolar globalist project. This opposition, which is different from simple negation or conservatism, has a creative character. We understand the inevitability of some definite historical processes: our aim is to be aware of them, to take part in them, and to lead them in the direction that corresponds to our ideals.

It might be said that Eurasianism is the philosophy of multipolar globalization, appealing to all the societies and peoples of the Earth to build an original and authentic world, every component of which organically derives from historical traditions and local cultures.

Historically, the first Eurasianist theories made their appearance among Russian thinkers at the beginning of the twentieth century. However, those ideas were consonant with the spiritual and philosophical quest of all the peoples on Earth — at least, of those who realized the limited and inadequate nature of banal dogmas, as well as the failure and the blind alley to which the intellectual clichés of the time were bound. They spoke to the need to escape from the usual frameworks toward new horizons. Today we can attribute to Eurasianism a new, global meaning; we can realize how our Eurasianist work is not solely the work of the Russian school, even though it is often identified as such. It is also part of an enormous cultural and intellectual stratum belonging to all the peoples on Earth, not strictly corresponding to the narrow frame of what until recently, in the twentieth century, was considered immutable orthodoxy — namely the belief that all political ideals had to correspond to one of the liberal, Marxist, or nationalist models.

In this highest and broadest meaning, Eurasianism acquires a new and extraordinary significance. Now it is not only the form of the national idea for the new, post-Communist Russia, as it was considered by the founding fathers of the movement and even of the contemporary neo-Eurasianists in its initial stages. It is as a vast program of planetary and universal relevance, by far exceeding the borders of Russia and the Eurasian continent. In the same way as the concept of "Americanism" today may be applied to geographical regions found outside the borders of the American continent, Eurasianism denotes a distinct civilizational, cultural, philosophical, and strategic choice, which can be made by any individual, regardless of where on the planet he lives or to whichever national and spiritual culture he belongs.

In order to provide this interpretation of Eurasianism with real meaning, there is still much to be done. And to the extent that new cultural, national, philosophical, and religious strata will continue to join in our project, this global meaning of Eurasianism will be broadened, enriched, and changed in its features. Yet such an evolution of Eurasianist thinking must not remain simply a theoretical issue. Many aspects will only find their expression and accomplishment through concrete political practice.

In the Eurasianist synthesis, it is not the case that word can be thought without action, nor action without word.

The field of the spiritual battle for the sense and outcome of history is the whole world. The choice of one's camp belongs to everyone individually. Time will decide of the rest. Yet sooner or later, through great accomplishments and at the cost of dramatic battles, the hour of Eurasia shall come.

The Eurasianist Vision II

The structure of the International Eurasian Movement

The structure of the International Eurasian Movement is determined by its goals for the world as well as the current, unprecedented historical conditions. The main strategic goal of the Movement is the coordination of all Eurasian powers into a united sociopolitical front. This means the coordination, consolidation, and integration of all movements, tendencies, political and social organizations, institutions, funds, and so on that adhere to the goal of a multipolar world and of blossoming variety against unipolar globalization and the expansion of Atlanticism.

These Eurasian (in the broadest sense of the term) powers vary greatly, from powerful international organizations (e.g., the United Nations, which is doomed to fade away due to American hegemony), governmental institutions, and political parties to small groups of people who are united by common political, cultural, national, religious, and professional criteria.

Because there is such a diversity of potential participants, the structure of the Movement must be flexible and completely different from what is usually understood by a political party, movement, research center, governmental institution, or economic consortium.

The foundation of a multipolar world is an unprecedented task that mankind has never faced before. This new international struggle demands management in all spheres (the global communication networks, new technologies, transport, social and economic structures, etc.), including in its organizational aspects.

The effectiveness of our actions lies in the flexible and adaptive structure of the Movement. For example, open democracy and international activities correlate with the implementation of the projects of Eurasian development, religious organizations work with political structures on the basis of cooperation and dialogue, centers of economic cooperation led by Eurasian transnational corporations collaborate with military institutions, and so on.

All aspects of the Movement's activity represent a diversified system of relations: economics connected with politics, technology with ecology, information systems with culture, religious problems with military ones, strategic potential with industrial advances and administrative organization, and the advance of intellectuals along with mechanisms to create elites. Such a complex approach, amalgamating different spheres of human activity, is the central and unique aspect of the International Eurasian Movement as an innovative form of social existence.

Modern Atlanticist structures — "charity" foundations, research centers, and the combined mass media of the world — represent tangible instruments of the opposing ideological system, and have one goal: the creation of a unipolar world, led by the United States and the other "golden billion" countries. We are currently experiencing not only general patterns of development, a "spontaneous process," or a "theory without practice," but also a developed, powerful, and effective mechanism for the realization of any goal set by the adepts of Atlanticism and globalization.

Atlanticism is not just a theory. It includes NATO, the economic potential of most of the developed countries of the world, the controlled global mass media, a network of think tanks across the world which provide ideological support, and countless other agents of influence, as represented in international organizations, political parties, religious bodies, and so on. All these are the instruments called upon to establish and strengthen the unipolar world.

Eurasianism must develop a similarly effective and ideologically and organizationally centralized structure to unite the adversaries of globalization. Globalization has passed beyond the boundaries of the US and the Western world: today we can talk about an "Atlanticist international." The historical mission of Eurasianism lies in the creation of a common basis for the struggle and the attempt to establish a different vision of the future — a multipolar and just one. We must implement an equivalent structure, the Eurasian International, with the long-term goal of coordinating activity in support of multipolarity.

The Eurasian Movement and the project of the Eurasian continental belt

The International Eurasian Movement considers the Russian Federation to be its main launching pad and the main base for its activity. The reason for is that, for centuries, Russia has sought an alternative to the Western model of social development, from the conflict between the Russian Orthodox Church and the Catholic and Protestant churches, to further opposition beginning in the Middle Ages and lasting until the end of the nineteenth century, and finally the confrontation between two global socioeconomic systems in the twentieth century. Throughout her history, Russia has tried to realize its alternative ethical ideals — sometimes with tragic consequences.

Russian history has not come to its end, and the Russian people remain devoted to their historical mission, which is why Russia is destined to become the leader of a new global, Eurasian alternative to the Western vision of the world's future. Eurasianism offers a plan for a new global sociopolitical organization for all the peoples of the Earth. The development of the Eurasian organization can happen all over the world at the same time, anywhere globalization faces opposition. Any manifestation of such opposition is vital for Russian politics and the Eurasian process as a whole across the world. Additionally, the implementation of Eurasian reforms in the Russian Federation could be very important to adherents of multipolarity throughout the world.

In real-world politics, the International Eurasian Movement must support the creation of four geo-economical zones. The fourth geo-economic zone is the Eurasian continental belt. Atlanticist geo-economics proposes only three zones and calls Eurasia the "black hole," or a territory that is partly owned by the other three zones. Thus, the integration of this territory is the most important stage in the implementation of Eurasian geo-economic and geopolitical prerequisites. Therefore, if the other three zones — the American, Euro-African and Pacific — are to be transformed according to Eurasian principles, the Eurasian continental belt must first be created.

The Eurasian continental belt proposes the rapid economic and strategic integration of each of the four Great Spaces of the globe. First, there must be a political and economic consolidation of each of these spaces, which today consist of one or more nation-states. The boundaries of India and China reach the limits of their

Great Spaces, but for Russia, the CIS countries, and the continental Muslim countries (Iran, Pakistan, Afghanistan, and possibly Turkey, Iraq, and Syria) integration is a very complicated process. The foundation of these Great Spaces is the primary goal of the Eurasian movement. The integration of the Great Spaces may occur parallel to the construction of the Eurasian continental belt. Success in one direction will boost progress in another.

Joint activity — economic, strategic, political, and diplomatic — between the countries of the Eurasian continent is happening a lot today, which is why we will very soon be able to proclaim the Eurasian continental belt project for a united geo-economic and strategic system for collective continental security. Moreover, all its participants are long-standing adherents of the idea of a multipolar world. In the past, they formed the framework of the "socialist camp" or numbered among the Third World countries in the non-aligned movement. Both stand for their own future as against absorption into the project of unipolar globalization. The main goal of the International Eurasian Movement is to promote this process, properly substantiate it, and boost the foundation for necessary political, strategic, and diplomatic institutions, as well as international economic structures, funds, and corporations. We must also promote cooperation between these nations, taking into consideration their historical, religious, and ethnic factors.

The Eurasian model of political integration into Great Spaces provides an opportunity to resolve conflicts and cooperate on the basis of understanding and harmony. The successful use of the Eurasian model will solve ethnic as well as other conflicts within the Russian Federation (especially in the Caucasus) and will prove itself to be of great value to the countries of the CIS (especially Karabakh, Kyrgyzstan, and Tajikistan). The intensive use of the Eurasian model in Russia and the CIS will lead to the rapid creation of the Eurasian Union, the Great Spaces, and the Eurasian continental belt.

The American belt

The indisputable domination of the North American Great Space, consisting of the US and Canada, must proceed by beginning the intergration processes with Latin America, which consists of two Great Spaces: South and Central America. This process must preserve the historical, economic, and political qualities of Latin civilization, which are different from those of the Anglo-Saxons. This presumes wider civilizational independence for Latin American countries than has been traditionally permitted by the leader of this meridian zone, namely the US. This theory of Eurasian integration of close civilizations and cultural spaces will be able to guarantee fully-fledged development to the nations of Latin America, which will promote its geopolitical status and bring about harmonious solutions to its ethnic, social, technological, ecological, demographic, and economic problems.

In the American geo-economic belt, Eurasianism supports the following:

❊ the limitation of American strategic, political and economic interests to the boundaries of the American meridian zone; our allies in this question will be the American conservatives, who are adherents of both isolationism and expansionism as limited by the Monroe Doctrine;

❊ maximum autonomy for democratic, ecological, and national-cultural movements;

❊ the integration of Latin countries into Central and South American Great Spaces, which will strengthen their cultural autonomy.

Today, America's influence is the most negative tendency in the world as it brings Atlanticism to all the corners of the Earth. This judgment can be understood when one understands that America promotes unipolar globalization and acts as the world's policeman. This situation will change, however, when America rejects its current plans for world hegemony and agrees to become a regional superpower within the limits of the American meridian zone alone. We also cannot rule out the possibility that, after cultural suppression is eliminated, other nations will objectively reconsider the values of American civilization and might adopt those elements of it that they consider positive. Thus, the US can multiply its adherents without having to resort to oppression or force. The Eurasian goal for this meridian zone is to search for proponents of the Eurasian viewpoint within the United States and Latin America.

The Euro-African belt

The European Union is rapidly becoming the economic leader of the Euro-African Great Space, and it plans to promote its strategic and geopolitical status in the both the middle- and long-term period (Eurocorps, a common European security policy, etc.). Integration in Europe is the expression of Eurasian logic (with the exception of regionalists, who promote democratic and traditional orientations).

The Eurasian project for the EU is its qualitative leap towards the Euro-African Great Space. The stages of European integration are sure signs of Eurasianism: the rejection of nation-states, a common economic and currency system, and the step-by-step independence of the EU from American domination.

Asia presents its strategic will for a multipolar world along with its poor material resources. Europe possesses an integrated geo-economic system; however, until recently we have not seen any declarations regarding the importance of a multipolar world. The International Eurasian Movement is very interested in the further development of the integration of a united Europe, as well as the preservation of the principles of Europe's inner, organic multipolarity. But Europe must stop its promotion of the idea of the individual as an atom. The European nations must turn to tradition and renew Europe's great culture, in spite of its immersion in the primitive clichés of Americanism.

Eurasianism supports the strengthening of the regional strategic, economic, and political status of the EU and believes that it is able to become the geopolitical leader of the Euro-African belt. This process has two vectors, the first being the development of European-Muslim relations, and the second being European-African relations (especially regarding sub-Saharan Africa). Having independence in solving Euro-Arab and Euro-American issues will give the EU an opportunity to become a powerful player in the multipolar world.

The foundation of the Euro-African meridian zone will eliminate resource dependence, but if Europe tries to become the dominant power in the South, it will clash with the interests and hegemony of the United States. Preventing the EU from stretching into the South is imperative for the Americans to retain control over Europe. The Eurasian project aims for the disintegration of the trans-Atlantic power structure and promotes strong and mutually advantageous cooperation with Africa.

The second Great Space here is the Arab world, stretching from Muslim North Africa to the countries of the Maghreb and the Middle East. This is a very complicated region that falls within the historical boundaries of the Ottoman Empire. These territories must be integrated into one geopolitical structure that will establish economic and political relations between Europe and Saharan Africa. The fact that these territories are under the domination of Islamic traditions may be an additional factor in integration. There are some forms of Islamic radicalism — those that pretend to be universal — that oppose the basic Eurasian principles of cultural diversity and a system of autonomies (Eurasian blossoming variety). Thus, the main Eurasian allies in the Arab world who adhere to Islam and also respect local traditions are the Sufi Tariqas, Shi'ites, and those ethnic groups in the region who promulgate spiritual and cultural diversity.

Another danger is the attempts of Islamic extremists to expand into non-Arab Islamic regions, from Turkey to Kazakhstan and the Philippines. These efforts are typically led by Atlanticist-oriented regimes (e.g., Saudi Arabia). This tendency must be strongly opposed.

A very important goal for Eurasianism is the strategic integration of Saharan Africa and its transformation into an independent Great Space. The borders of almost every African country were inherited from colonial times. They do not fit the historical, ethnic, cultural, or economic conditions of the African nations. The fragmentary and artificial state system there is the cause of many of its ethnic problems and of crypto-colonialism. The African people's psychological type is better suited to the ideas of Eurasianism, because the Eurasian Idea is open to a sense of wholeness and the organic integration of people, history, society, and nature. Freedom from Africa's post-colonial heritage is possible only through integration into a single strategic civilization that is friendly with the Arab world and oriented towards a united Europe, which will be the leader of the Euro-African meridian zone. Special attention must be paid to Israel, which plays an important role as an Atlanticist agent in the region. We need to work out a new model for stopping the Arab-Israeli conflict and propose a positive formula for their participation in the construction of this zone.

The Pacific belt

The strategic, political, and economic leader of the Pacific belt must be Japan, a unique civilization comprised of a small group of islands and an outstanding example of the concentration of a Great Space in a very small geographical area. Japan has enormous potential for expansion, a very strict social order, and great vigor. Japanese potential, which has been artificially restrained by the US and has only been realized in the economic sphere, must be freed and used for the reorganization of the entire Pacific zone.

Japan, just as Europe in the Euro-African zone, is the objective leader of the Pacific. Independence from American domination in the geopolitical, political and military senses is a necessary condition for the implementation of real multipolarity.

Japan, like Europe, currently belongs to the Atlanticist sphere of influence, but it has great potential and the right type of national psychology to become the frame for the Pacific meridian zone. This country needs Eurasian support in the economic and strategic spheres. Any strengthening of this country automatically increases the overall potential of Eurasianism.

Other potential Great Spaces of the Pacific belt are the Malay archipelago and some countries on the Indochina peninsula. They represent a complex system of technological progress, due to their inclusion in the global capitalist system, but retain many elements of traditional society.

It is very important for the political elites of this region to consider the present situation as "potential Eurasianism," because Eurasian philosophy is based on an organic adherence to tradition combined with technological advance and social development. Australia and New Zealand must be integrated into the civilizational and geo-economic context of Greater Asia and be freed from their colonialist heritage of the twentieth century. Australian Eurasianism is the creation of a new model of relations between European Anglo-Saxons and an increasing number of immigrants from Asia (Chinese, Vietnamese, Malay, etc.).

Towards the Eurasian Union through the Eurasian process

Transition from the nation-state model to the Great Space model must proceed on different levels on the basis of a multidimensional integration. These levels are the economic, geopolitical, strategic, political, cultural, informational, and linguistic. Each of these levels provide their own political action model for the International Eurasian Movement.

Special attention must be paid to the process of the transformation of the CIS into the Eurasian Union. The CIS is an example of an asymmetrical group of nation-states in which one of them, the Russian Federation, has the right to partial geopolitical sovereignty, while the others do not have such a right. The Great Space that must be created on the basis of this group of nation-states is the Eurasian Union, which will be similar to the European Union — a political organizational structure with centralized economic and strategic administration systems.

The creation of the Eurasian Union is the central objective of the International Eurasian Movement, which will initiate, control, and coordinate the Eurasian process to achieve this goal. The Eurasian process is the multidimensional evolution of governmental, economic, political, industrial, strategic, and cultural institutions of each of the member states of the CIS into a new political and strategic formation, the Eurasian Union.

The creation of this Union is of the utmost importance, and is not simply a declaration. The legal framework of the Union must be preceded by a prolonged, fundamental integration process. Before we announce the implementation of a new international power structure, we must establish a proper, flexible administrative system to support the entire process. For this, we will use the example of the European Union.

The basis of this administrative system must be international, which is necessary in order to coordinate integration. This integration must be directed by the International Eurasian Movement and its representative offices in the CIS. We can temporarily call it the "headquarters of the Eurasian process." All activity must be coordinated with the bodies of the central governments: the President, the presidential administration, parliament, the wider government, the Eurasian Economic Community, the Public Accord for Collective Security, and so on.

The main goal of this headquarters will be the elaboration and realization of integration projects, which will not necessarily be considered official initiatives of the government. Initiatives may be undertaken by social organizations, such as the Eurasian Movement and so on, that promote their programs broadly and which can be relied upon by all state governments and their security services.

The Eurasian Union is not simply an association of different states followed by the dissolution of national administrations, nor is it an enlarged version of the Russian Federation with its governmental, administrative, and political institutions. It presumes a completely new administrative system, and the evolution of old as well as the creation of new bodies, which is why the CIS governments are unable even to formulate the objectives of Eurasian integration.

The structure of the International Eurasian Movement includes a system of funds, consortiums, banks and stock systems, media holdings, scientific and educational institutions, and strategic and geopolitical research centers. These will lend themselves to the acceleration of the process of Eurasian integration. The International Eurasian Movement, which is critical for the coordination of integration, must qualitatively differ from common political parties, social organizations, inter-governmental commissions, or purely economic communities. Existing elements of political administration can cooperate with the Movement but cannot replace it. New challenges require new means, because the integration process will demand the transformation of the existing elements of the nation-states and of the societies.

Autonomy as the Basic Principle of Eurasian Nationhood

Sovereignty or autonomy

The current structure of national power in the Russian Federation, which is based on the principle of the sovereignty of its subjects, is deeply flawed. The situation has been aggravated by the policy, which was favored by Yeltsin, of "take as much sovereignty as you can," which has been implemented over the course of the last decade and been directed to render federal subjects with as many of the attributes of sovereignty as possible. Local elites interpreted that policy as an invitation to *laissez-faire* type lawlessness. In fact, that approach would condemn Russia to disintegration in the course of an inevitable "parade of sovereignties." That was graphically demonstrated by the examples of Chechnya and of Tatarstan, in a milder version.

The problem is that sovereignty by definition cannot be sustained in a restricted form: it always tends toward totality (independence in the realm of foreign affairs, the military, its own currency, etc.). An accepted concept in classical political science is that sovereignty supposes an alienated territory and ultimate domination over such. In the circumstances of the Russian Federation, that means actual renunciation — albeit somewhat gradual — of the principle of the unity and indivisibility of Russia. As a matter of fact, the federal model is efficient only in homogeneous societies. For such a complicated, asymmetric, heterogeneous, unevenly populated and multicultural entity such as Russia, an entirely different principle is necessary. The idea of autonomy is to become that principle.

Parameters of autonomy

Autonomy does not allow for the presence of sovereignty, or in general, any attributes of nationhood. Autonomy is self-rule, nothing more. Issues of strategy, foreign relations, and strategic planning fall outside the autonomy's competency. Meanwhile a multitude of issues that are currently under the jurisdiction of federal authority and regulated by federal legislation (civil and administrative law, the judicial system, the management of the economy, and other activities) could be delegated to the autonomies.

The major distinction of autonomies from how the subjects of the Russian Federation exist today is that in autonomy, the subject is not a territorial, quasi-national entity, but a community of people unified by some common trait.

Autonomies can be of any size, from several families to entire peoples. Large autonomies may contain smaller autonomies within their boundaries. Overall, the idea of community is at the basis of its societal structure.

Types of autonomy

* Autonomy of nationalities. Emerges within the framework of a people, having been shaped into a historical entity and possessing certain traditions of self-governance and composed of a single body invulnerable to erosion.

* Ethnic autonomy. Suitable for peoples with no features of nationality.

* Theocratic autonomy. Emerges among nations with a high degree of religious consciousness, in which religious institutions are involved in the internal management of the society, thus partly embodying the real power within a given society (judicial, administrative, etc.).

* Religious autonomy. Suitable for communities formed along religious lines, in which religion is not involved in the internal management of the society.

The four types of autonomy mentioned above may converge, forming national-theocratic, ethno-religious, or other types of autonomy.

* Cultural-historical autonomy. Incorporates historically shaped communities of people unified by a common mentality and culture. Examples are the Cossacks and the Pomors of northern Russia.

✳ Social-industrial autonomy. This form of autonomy is mostly applicable to recently-inhabited territories; as a rule it develops around enterprises that lead to the formation of towns or a national industrial complex. In the future it will be desirable that such autonomies evolve on the bases of socio-economic autonomies of other traditional types.

✳ Economic autonomy. A type of autonomy that forms in association with an existing one, which guarantees them special treatment in those spheres that are regulated by federal legislation (legal exemptions or modifications for the needs of specific territories, tax relief, relaxed customs duties, etc.).

✳ Linguistic autonomy. This type reflects linguistic commonality among representatives of various autonomies. May transcend as well as encompass autonomies of other traditional types.

✳ Communal autonomy. An autonomy otherwise devoid of integrating features, which nevertheless brings together people cohabitating within the same territorial limits and/or employed in the same field. Examples are traditional ancestral-tribal entities or ecological settlements comprised of former city-dwellers.

✳ Some territories where no communities of any kind have formed (unpopulated or scarcely-populated lands) may be declared federal lands, i.e., territories where only federal legislation and federal regulatory acts are enforceable.

Autonomies and the federal center

Unlike the current subjects of the Russian Federation, autonomies could possess significantly greater rights in the cultural realm, day-to-day affairs, administration, legal issues, and proprietary management. In fact, the functions of the courts of law, the law enforcement agencies, management, and control could be delegated to the autonomies. Federal legislation should only regulate the smallest number of matters that are common to all the autonomies in its purview. Federal courts of law and federal law enforcement agencies should only be concerned with conflicts of an intercommunal nature. All intracommunal issues should be resolved internally, in accordance with established traditions that have been inscribed into local laws. In turn, autonomies delegate the right to decide matters related to national security, international relations, and strategic planning to the federal authorities. All the remaining vestiges of sovereignty at the local level should be eradicated.

The new Eurasian structure of the state, rooted in the principle of autonomy, also implies a certai mutation of the federal organs of power.

A congress of the autonomies, comprised of the best representatives from the more significant autonomies in the country, should become the institution to make the primary strategic decisions of the state. The federal organs of power (the Eurasian administration) should be composed of leaders and the most respected representatives of the autonomies. The autonomies will also delegate representatives for service in the common armed forces and the federal law enforcement agencies. Since the majority of issues will be decided at the local level, the federal bureaucratic apparatus will become quite small.

Thus, the Western system of formal, electoral democracy, which has deteriorated into a criminal system of fraud and the corruption of the electorate in Russia, will be replaced by an organic democracy which mandates creative participation by the best representatives of the communities in the national government. This type of democracy — democracy by the citizenry, not by the mob — is characteristic of ancient Greece and modern Switzerland.

Land use in autonomies

An essential issue is land use. None of the autonomies should have a right to alienate any other territory. The core principle should be: the proprietor of the land is the Creator. Generally, land should be revered, and a cult of the Motherland of sorts should be revived. All land will be under the collective ownership of the entire people of Russia and managed by the leadership of Russia. Autonomies will be provided those parcels of land that are currently occupied by them, and which can be used by them free of charge. The very concept of a "border" within the Russian state (and, in a larger perspective, throughout the entire Eurasian universe) should be replaced by the concept of a "boundary." A boundary is a nominal line, with no legal significance; a line along which territories used by one community are connected to territories used by another community. Boundaries shall be flexible, not fixed. Borders are used to divide; boundaries are to bind.

The principle of autonomy itself, as opposed to the principle of sovereignty, envisions subjects not as territories with arbitrarily drawn, oftentimes contested borders, but as human beings with a distinct national and religious identity — fully-fledged members of a collective entity. Thus, the substitution of the principle of sovereignty by that of autonomy makes separatist movements and border disputes unfeasible within the Russian Federation. The term "federation" itself may then be abolished. The state acquires stability, and the peoples of Russia gain a unique opportunity for social development.

Autonomies and megalopises

Major cities are the most problematic zones for the application of the principle of autonomy. City-dwellers are the least connected with their national and religious traditions. They also lack a connection to the land. They are the most preoccupied by the processes of Westernization and globalization. Besides which the emergence of large cities, a common occurrence in Europe or Japan where land is in short supply, looks very strange in Russia, given the abundance of her uncultivated territories. All this suggests that major cities should be gradually depopulated. The main manufacturing industries should be relocated out of the cities. Regarding residential areas, a system of townships (*sloboda*) should be implemented. Townships are ecological settlements separated from the cities by clean forests, where communities should be formed according to ethnic, religious, cultural-historic, or other principles (a special mention here should be made of the experience of "compatriot communities"). Thus, the organs of management, cultural institutions and the service sector are to remain within the current city limits. In Moscow some examples of the implementation of the *sloboda* principle are already visible. The leadership of Moscow encourages self-governance within a single residential building or on a block. This allows for the effective resolution of many problems, but most importantly, the communalization of a megalopolis is taking place: the people are learning to be a part of a specific community and to act in concert. In the future, the majority of matters in a *sloboda* will be decided internally.

Autonomies and "hot spots"

If the transition from the sovereignty of its subjects to the principle of autonomy might be postponed throughout most of Russia, or perhaps conducted at a slow pace (which nevertheless is extremely dangerous), then such a transition should be implemented immediately in Russia's "hot spots," and in the hot spots throughout the CIS.

An analysis of the causes of the bloody interethnic conflicts in Russia, such as those in Chechnya, the Prigorodny region of Vladikavkaz, and so on, clearly exposes the fateful role played by the terrible idea of local sovereignty.

The regions of the different ethnic populations interconnect in such a complicated pattern that drawing correct borderlines between them is practically impossible. The idea of sovereignty draws the local elites toward acquiring more and more of the attributes of nationhood, including stricter borders. All this leads to situations that are rife with conflict and which cannot be resolved within the old paradigm. A new and qualitatively different concept is necessary. The concept of autonomy negates sovereignty and all its attributes. Instead, people, not territories with their problem-ridden borders, play the role of the subject. Autonomy thus presents a unique opportunity for "exiting the dead end."

Russia is a unique multinational, multiconfessional, and multicultural universe with huge uninhabited territories, diverse landscapes, and a multitude of communities with their own historical traditions which vary widely in their mentality and ways of life. Applying patterns developed in a very different historical context to this reality can be anything but smooth and efficient. The implementation of the classical, federal model in Russia is a time bomb which could tear our country apart into bloody pieces. It is necessary to find a model adaptable to the unique features of Russia, one which would guarantee sound national and cultural development, religious revival, and peace and prosperity for the peoples of Russia.

In our view, the substitution of the principle of sovereignty by that of autonomy is absolutely urgent. There can be no alternative to autonomy.

The International Eurasian Movement

The International Eurasian Movement is a Non-Governmental Organization (NGO) with branches in 22 countries including all countries of the CIS, in the EU (Germany, France, Italy, and Great Britain), in the Americas (the United States and Chile), in the Islamic countries (Lebanon, Syria, Egypt, Turkey, Iran, and Pakistan), in the Far East (India, Japan, and Vietnam) and so on. In the Russian Federation there are 56 regional representatives of the Eurasian Movement.

The International Eurasian Movement was officially created in a constitutional congress that was held in Moscow on November 20, 2003 and is registered with the Russian Ministry of Juridical Affairs as the International Social Movement, actualizing its goals on a global scale and in every country where the activities of an international NGO is accepted.

The main goals of the International Eurasian Movement are:

✳ the common struggle for a multipolar world, based on the cooperation of different peoples, civilizations, and cultures for peace and mutual prosperity;

✳ a close partnership between the European and Asiatic countries, with a special role reserved for Russia as the primary mediator of this process;

✳ the integration of the post-Soviet space to the point of the creation of a united "Eurasian Alliance" in the cultural, economic, informational, strategic, and political fields;

✳ an active and multilateral dialogue between the traditional confessions and the ethnoses of Eurasia, as well as mutual understanding and respect between the various Eurasian societies and their elites;

❋   the conservation of the cultural, religious, and ethnic identities of every
     people, and the further development of the uniqueness and originality of
     each;

❋   the strengthening of peace and order based on Eurasian principles — Pax
     Eurasiatica;

❋   opposition toward the negative tendencies abound in the world, including
     unipolar and unidimensional globalization, cultural degradation, terrorism,
     narcotics traffic, the lack of social justice, and both ecological and demo-
     graphic catastrophes.

The activities of the Eurasian Movement are coordinated by the resolutions of its
Higher Council.

    The executive organ of the Eurasian Movement is the Eurasian Committee,
which has its headquarter in Moscow.

    The President of the Eurasian Committee and the leader of the Eurasian Move-
ment is Alexander Dugin, the philosopher and founder of neo-Eurasianism, and
the creator of the modern Russian school of geopolitics.

The Eurasian Economic Club

The purpose of the activities of the Eurasian Economic Club

The purpose of the activities of the Eurasian Economic Club are:

✳ to develop economic partnerships between the business organizations of the Eurasian continent;

✳ to support the development of commercial relations among these countries;

✳ to promote the integration of the Eurasian continent into united economic space.

The support of Eurasian initiatives

The Eurasian Economic Club considers Eurasianism as a fruitful ideological base upon which to strengthen the economic network in both the East and the West. The primary goal of the Club's activities are to help to bolster Eurasian initiatives and thinking in the realms of economics, culture, science, and interconfessional relations.

The main principles of the Club's activities

The Eurasian Economic Club has chosen the following goals as its primary focus:

✳ the development of a partnership in the field of energy resources (oil, gas, and so on);

✳ the planning and implementation of transportation projects;

﹡ collaboration in the financial sector, including in banking and the issuing of securities;

﹡ cooperation in the sphere of communications and information systems;

﹡ the execution of joint construction projects;

﹡ legal consultation for business transactions and the evaluation of risks involving each country;

﹡ business consulting which takes into account special geopolitical factors;

﹡ trade.

The primary regions of concern to the Eurasian Economic Club

The Club focuses particular attention on the countries of the CIS and works particularly toward the promotion of economic interactions between them — such projects as the Eurasian common market, its customs union, and so on.

The Club considers efforts towards a greater economic partnership with the countries of the EU to be of the utmost importance.

The Club also wishes to promote business partnerships with the countries of Asia.

The Greater Europe Project

A Geopolitical Draft of a Future Multipolar World

1. Following the decline and disappearance of the socialist East European bloc at the end of the last century, a new vision of world geopolitics based on a new approach became a necessity. But the inertia of political thinking and the lack of historical imagination among the political elites of the victorious West has led to a simplistic course: the conceptual basis of Western-style liberal democracy, a market economy, and the strategic domination of the United States throughout the world became the only solution to all kinds of emerging challenges, and was held to be a universal model that it should be all of humanity's imperative to accept.

2. Before our eyes this new reality is emerging: the reality of a world organized entirely in accordance with the American paradigm. An influential neoconservative think tank in the US openly refers to it by a more appropriate term — the "global empire" (sometimes "benevolent empire," as per Robert Kagan). This empire is unipolar and concentric by its very nature. In the center there is the "rich North" and the Atlanticist community. The rest of the world is dismissed as the zone of underdeveloped or developing countries, and is considered peripheral. These countries are presumed to be moving in the same direction and to be taking the same course as the core countries of the West had long before.

3. In keeping with this unipolar vision, Europe is seen as the outskirts of America, the world capital, and as a bridgehead of the American West on the Eurasian continent. Europe is considered to be part of the rich North, and yet not as a leader — rather as a junior partner without proper interests or specific

characteristics of its own. Europe, in light of such a project, is perceived as an object and not the subject, and as a geopolitical entity deprived of its autonomous identity and will, and of real and acknowledged sovereignty. Most of the cultural, political, ideological, and geopolitical particularity of European heritage is thought of as something passé: anything that was once valued as useful has already been integrated into the global Western project; what's left over is discounted as irrelevant. In such circumstances Europe becomes geopolitically denuded, deprived of its own proper and independent self. Being located next to regions with diverse, non-European civilizations, and with its own identity weakened or even completely negated by the approach of the global American empire, Europe can easily lose its own cultural and political shape.

4. However, liberal democracy and the free market account for only part of Europe's historical heritage. There have been other possibilities proposed and other issues dealt with by great European thinkers, scientists, politicians, ideologists and artists. Europe's identity is much wider and deeper than the simplistic American ideological fast-food of the global empire complex, with its caricaturist mixture of ultra-liberalism, free market ideology and democracy based on quantity over quality. In the era of the Cold War, the unity of the Western world on both sides of the Atlantic had a more or less solid basis in terms of the mutual defense of its common values. But now this threat is no longer present and the old rhetoric doesn't work anymore. It should be revised and new arguments supplied. There is no longer a clear common foe who genuinely poses an existential threat to the West, and a positive basis for a united West in the future is almost totally lacking. As a consequence, European countries are beginning to make social choices that stand in stark contrast to the Anglo-Saxon — today American — striving towards ultra-liberalism.

5. Present-day Europe has its own strategic interests that differ substantially from American interests and from the needs of the project of Western globalization. Europe has its own particular and positive attitude towards its southern and eastern neighbors. In some cases, Europe's economic needs, its need for energy resources, and its strategy for a common defense initiative don't coincide at all with their American counterparts.

6. These general considerations lead us, who are European intellectuals deeply concerned about the fate of our cultural and historical Motherland of Europe, to the conclusion that we badly need an alternative vision of the world's future where the place, role and mission of Europe and of European civilization would be different, greater, better, and more secure than it is within the frame of the global empire project, with its all-too-evident features of imperialism.

7. The only feasible alternative under the present circumstances is to be found in the context of a multipolar world. Multipolarity can grant the right and the freedom to develop its own potential, to organize its own domestic reality in accordance with the specific identity of its culture and people, and to propose a reliable basis for just and balanced international relations amongst the world's nations to any country or civilization on the planet. Multipolarity should be based on the principle of equity among the various kinds of political, social, and economic organizations of these nations and states. Technological progress and a growing openness between countries should promote dialogue amongst, and the prosperity of, all peoples and nations, but at the same time it shouldn't endanger their respective identities. Differences between civilizations do not have to necessarily culminate in an inevitable clash between them, in contrast to the simplistic logic of some American writers. Dialogue, or rather "polylogue," is a realistic and feasible possibility that we should all exploit in this regard.

8. Concerning Europe directly, and in contrast to other plans for the creation of something "greater" in the old-fashioned, imperialistic sense of the word — be it the Greater Middle East Project or the pan-nationalist plan for a Greater Russia or a Greater China — we suggest, as a concrete manifestation of the multipolar approach, a balanced and open vision of a Greater Europe as a new concept for the future development of our civilization in its strategic, social, cultural, economic, and geopolitical dimensions.

9. Greater Europe will consist of the territory contained within the boundaries that coincide with the limits of European civilization. This kind of boundary is something completely new, as is the concept of the civilization-state. The nature of these boundaries presumes a gradual transition — not an abrupt demarcation. Therefore, this Greater Europe should be open for interaction with its neighbors to the west, the east or the south.

10. A Greater Europe in the general context of a multipolar world is conceived of as being surrounded by other great territories, each of which bases their respective unities on the affinity of civilizations between the nations of which they are comprised. We can thus predict the eventual appearance of a Greater North America, a Greater Eurasia, a Greater Pacific Asia and, in the more distant future, a Greater South America and a Greater Africa. No country — except the United States — can afford to defend its true sovereignty by relying solely on its own resources in the world today. No one of them could be considered as an autonomous pole capable of counterbalancing the Atlanticist power. Thus, multipolarity demands a large-scale integration process. It could be called a "chain of globalizations" — but globalization within concrete limits — coinciding with the approximate boundaries of various civilizations.

11. We imagine this Greater Europe as a sovereign geopolitical power, with its own strong cultural identity, with its own social and political options based on the principles of the European democratic tradition, with its own defensive capabilities (including nuclear weapons), and with its own strategic access to energy and mineral resources. All this would allow it to make its own decisions regarding peace or war with other countries or civilizations completely independently. All of the above depends on a common European will as well as a democratic procedure for making decisions.

12. In order to promote our project of a Greater Europe and the multipolarity concept, we appeal to all the various political forces in the European nations, as well as to the Russians, the Americans, and the Asians, to reach beyond their usual political options, and beyond their cultural and religious differences, to actively support our initiative. We call for the creation of Committees for a Greater Europe, or other kinds of organizations sharing the multipolar approach, in any place where they can exist. These organizations must reject unipolarity and recognize the growing danger of American imperialism, and elaborate a similar concept for other civilizations. If we work together, strongly affirming each of our different identities, we will be able to found a balanced, just, and a better world, a Greater World where any worthy culture, society, faith, tradition, or act of human creativity will find its proper and rightful place.

Eurasian Keys to the Future

Excerpted from an interview conducted in 2012 in *Ziaristi Online*

At Moscow State University you are also the head of the Center for Conservative Studies. What is the purpose of creating such a Center? How important is the establishment of a conservative ideology in Russia, in your opinion?

I think conservatism is, first of all, a pronounced psychological constant of Russian society. Our society is conservative in all things, reacts poorly to change, and strives to keep some of its essential features intact. To examine the nature of these features, and to attach to this psychology a certain scientific rigor in examining it in its comprehensive philosophical, sociological, and political dimensions are the tasks set by the Center for Conservative Studies. Conservatism is a multidimensional and very diverse phenomenon; it is neither an answer nor a panacea to the problems we face. It's just a trend that takes shape in various ways in political and ideological terms. In this sense, the Center has a wide field of research. This non-profit initiative brings together academic researchers exploring this problem in practically all the major institutions of Russia. The Center publishes anthologies on philosophy, including on the Fourth Political theory, on Tradition (the *Tradition* almanac), on geopolitics (*Leviathan*), on the sociology of the imagination (*Imaginer*), and on ethnic issues (*Centrum*). The Center for Conservative Research is a world unto itself, a very complex intellectual and academic environment which includes a wide variety of components.

Pre-modern, modern, postmodern… How can this philosophical concept of yours be expressed in plain language? Meaning, where does Russia, the former Soviet Union, and the Black Sea-Caspian Sea region stand in these three historical paradigms, and where should they be, in your opinion?

Strictly speaking, pre-modern, modern, and postmodern are part of a classic system for the classification of different types of societies. What I mean is something different, like a graph of historical sociology which can be overlain on different types of societies to determine their structure. This is why pre-modern societies can also exist in our time in the same way that modern and postmodern societies can exist in our time. When we say pre-modern, modern, and postmodern, we are not saying what was, what is, and what will be. This is a wrong conception, because all these societies exist today. Some of them existed in the past, and some did not, meaning that this is a more complex sociological model.

In the West, the succession of these types of societies from one to another happened in a natural, easily observable manner. Therefore, it is by following the example of Western societies that we can see how these models alternated historically and how they grew out of one another. In fact, this is a classification scheme that only completely fits the structure of Western society and its history. When it comes to other societies, this scale can only be used with reservations and amendments. This is very important.

The West is in transition from the modern condition — a very well-established state of affairs, a complete one and well thought-out, which has extended all the way to the bottom of its social strata — to the postmodern condition.

Where is Russia? Like many other societies, except the Western ones, we are, of course, fundamentally behind. That is why modernization is urgent for us. This alone points to the fact that we are at a different point in our development: the issues that are relevant to us are not those that are relevant to the West. Therefore, we have a different understanding of what the structure of our society is. Here's an interesting point: in analyzing the methods of how we should define the place of our society and the societies of the majority of the post-Soviet states in these terms, I came to the conclusion that we are dealing with a complex, controversial model, a hybrid which I called "archeomodern." In other words, on the surface our society has many features of modern society. But behind this façade and behind the scenes of the supposedly modern (the fact that there is a Constitution, law, civil rights, a stock market, democracy, and so on) are hiding the real mechanisms of another society, one which is totally obsolete and governed by other laws and other norms. But nobody talks about it and nobody acknowledges it, so as a consequence a certain system of social slyness has appeared in which things, including in sociology, politics, and values, are not called by their actual names.

In other words, on one hand, we are clearly not modern in a fully-fledged sense. For us, it is still to come. On the other hand, our society is full of elements of the postmodern: Kseniya Sobchak,[1] the Internet, Twitter. But we use these postmodern structures in our own way. For the Russian and the post-Soviet peoples, the Internet and blogging are a completely different thing from what they are for Western Europeans. Accordingly, our citizens have developed a dual consciousness — that is, people in Russia who believe that they are modern are in reality archaic, and those who think about nothing might be postmodern in some respects and might be further along the scale. In a society that is archeomodern, temporary structures are organized differently than they are in Western societies. The past may actually be ahead of us, while the future is behind us. And the present might be absent or inadequate — inadequate, that is, from the point of view of Western sociology.

The primary law of Russian society is heterotelia. In sociology, heterotelia is when, to quote Viktor Chernomyrdin, "We want the best, but it turns out like usual." That is, at the level of the public sector, people set clearly defined and rational goals, but the result ends up being entirely different and clearly not what they had planned. For example, during the Khrushchev era, the plan was for Communism to develop and reach its final stage by 1980, but the outcome of this process ended up being the destruction of socialism. That was an example of heterotelia. Thus, the archeomodern is a field where heterotelia becomes the basic social law: no matter what we do, we get are guaranteed to get a different result.

What paradigm is applicable to the former Communist countries that have become part of the European Union? Where do they stand in terms of heterotelia?

First of all, Europe is a matrix of modernization. The problem is that this modernization overlays more archaic structures. In the countries of Eastern and Southern Europe, we encounter something similar to the archeomodern. But once they be-

---

1   Kseniya Sobchak (b. 1981) is a well-known Russian television personality who has also been active in the liberal opposition to Vladimir Putin.

come part of the EU space, they undergo a tremendous impact from the matrix of modernization. That is, in Europe everything is modern, up to its educational system and its linguistic practices. When a country enters the European Union, the influence of the European matrix is so strong that modernization occurs very intensively, which is absolutely impossible to achieve when one is situated at a certain distance from Europe, or when one has such wide territories as Russia, Kazakhstan, or Ukraine. Ukraine is a dimension that defies European modernization, even in the case of its full integration into Europe, simply because of its size, cultural traditions, and many other things: some of them can be assimilated by the modern European society that is transitioning into the postmodern, and others cannot.

The question of which countries or which spaces, which cultures, and which societies can be modernized, truly Europeanized, and included in the European Union, and which cannot, remains open. Turkey, for example, clearly doesn't fit because of its economic and political parameters. All the good things the Turks have, made them become quite European. But overall, the size of this society, its culture, and its qualitative characteristics do not fit Europe at all. Therefore, Turkey will never be in the EU: it is more likely for the EU to fall apart then to accept Turkey into its structure. As for post-Soviet countries like Ukraine, and especially Georgia or Moldova, I think it is a lost cause, because in the archeomodern societies in which the archaic character is very strong, modernization will last for centuries.

As for the overall modernization of Russia, I generally doubt that this is even theoretically possible, since it has such a broad territory, and such a culture and history. It's just impossible.

It is better to come back to where I started — to Eurasianism. Let us accept our uniqueness, our archaic elements, and our permanently conservative element as it is: we shouldn't run from it, hide it, be ashamed of it, or attempt to modernize it, but rather recognize it for what it is. Once it is recognized as such, we must give ourselves an honest answer as to who we are. If we are nothing more than an undermodernized Europe, a distorted Europe, a caricature of Europe — no one would desire to live in such a country. If we are bearers of a special destiny, we have in this archaic character some very original and profound dimensions that require understanding, just as the first Slavophiles and Eurasianists thought, then it makes all the difference. In that case it only remains for us to reveal it and rehabilitate it somehow, in order to offer an apologia of the Russian character through Eura-

sianism and within a multipolar system. There is a European model of development defined by these three models, but there is another one, too. And if we stop
measuring everything according to the standards of others — with the so-called
common, but in actuality European yardstick — then we will discover in ourselves
the most unexpected and unusual features that we never noticed before because we
were looking at ourselves through the eyes of others. In this way, I think, we can
get out of this situation.

As for the possibility of the integration of some of the other post-Soviet countries into Europe, I think it is impossible even for Moldavians because they are even
more archaic than the Romanians or the Russians. This is good because it speaks
to the uniqueness of their country and its culture. It is a positive thing, it is their
wealth, and there should be no shame in this archaism. Archaic? Let it be archaic.
It's great! It is a deep, contemplative, and beautiful culture. I love it very much.
Many Romanians will soon be traveling to Moldova because of the linguistic connections, searching for their roots and their identity, especially as Romania will
soon be experiencing the crisis of their Europeanism. Yes, their archaic character
turned out to be too deep and defies such integration, as opposed to some other
Eastern European countries. We must still face the archeomoderns in Eastern Europe.

THE FOURTH
POLITICAL
THEORY

Against the Postmodern World

The evil of unipolarity

The current world order is unipolar, with the global West at its center and having the United States at its core.

This type of unipolarity has geopolitical and ideological aspects. Its geopolitical side is the strategic dominance of the Earth by the North American hyperpower and the efforts of Washington to organize the planet in such a manner as to be able to rule it in accordance with its own national, imperialistic interests. This is bad because it deprives other states and nations of genuine sovereignty.

When it is left to only one authority to decide what is right and what is wrong, and who should be punished, this is a global dictatorship. I am convinced this is unacceptable. We should fight against it. If someone deprives us of our freedom, we have to react. And we will. The American empire should be destroyed, and sooner or later, it will be.

Ideologically, this unipolarity is based on modern and postmodern values that are openly anti-traditional in nature. I share the vision of René Guénon and Julius Evola, who considered modernity and the ideologies derived from it — individualism, liberal democracy, capitalism, and so on — to be the causes of the coming catastrophe of humanity, and the global domination of Western attitudes as the final degradation of the Earth. The West is approaching its end, and we should not let it pull all the rest of us into the abyss along with it.

Spiritually, globalization is the manifestation of the Grand Parody: the kingdom of the Antichrist. The United States is at the center of its expansion. American values pretend to be "universal" ones. In actuality they are a new form of ideological aggression against the multiplicity of cultures and traditions that still exist in the other parts of the world. I am resolutely opposed to those Western values that are essentially modern and postmodern in nature, and which are promulgated by the United States by force or by influence (Afghanistan, Iraq, Libya, and perhaps tomorrow, Syria and Iran).

Therefore, all traditionalists should be against the West and globalization, as well as against the imperialist politics of the United States. It is the only logical and meaningful position. Traditionalists and other partisans of traditional principles and values should oppose the West and defend the Rest (if the Rest shows some sign of conserving the Tradition, either in part or as a whole).

There are people in the West, and even in the US, who don't agree with the present state of things and who don't approve of modernity and postmodernity. They are the defenders of the spiritual tradition of the pre-modern West. They should join with us in our common struggle. They should take part in our revolt against the modern world. We would fight together against a common enemy.

Another question concerns the structure of this possible anti-globalist and anti-imperialist front, and its participants. I think we should welcome all those forces that struggle against the West, the US, liberal democracy, and modernity and postmodernity. Our common enemy necessitates all kinds of political alliances. Muslims, Christians, Russians, Chinese, Leftists, Rightists, Hindus, Jews — all who challenge the present state of things, and globalization in particular, should be our friends and allies. Let our ideals be different, but we share one very important thing in common: we hate our present reality. Our ideals differ only in terms of the specific vision that each of us wants to achieve, something that only has the potential to become a reality, but the challenge we are facing is already very real. This should be the basis of the new alliance. All those who view globalization, Westernization and postmodernization negatively should coordinate their efforts in the creation of a new strategy of resistance to this omnipresent evil. We can even find those who see things in the same way in the US as well — among those who choose Tradition as opposed to the present state of decadence.

To the Fourth Political Theory

At this point we should ask a very important question: what kind of ideology should we use to oppose globalization and its principles? I think that all the anti-liberal ideologies — Communism, socialism, and fascism — are not relevant anymore. They all tried to fight liberal capitalism and they failed. This is partly the case because, at the end of time, it is evil that prevails; partly it is also because of their inner contradictions and limitations. It is time to deeply revise the anti-liberal ideologies of the past.

What were their positive aspects? They can be seen in the fact that they were anti-capitalist and anti-liberal, as well as anti-cosmopolite and anti-individualist. These features should be accepted and integrated into the ideology of the future. However, Communist doctrine is modern, atheist, materialist, and cosmopolite. It should be thrown out. On the other hand, its advocacy of social solidarity, social justice, socialism itself, and a holistic approach to society are good aspects of this doctrine. We need to separate the materialistic and modernist aspects out of Communism and socialism, and reject them.

In the theories of Third Way — which were dear, to a certain point, to some traditionalists, such as Julius Evola — there were some unacceptable elements. First of all, there was racism, xenophobia, and chauvinism. These reflected not only moral failings but also theoretically and anthropologically inconsistent attitudes. The difference between ethnoses doesn't indicate either superiority or inferiority. These differences should be accepted and affirmed without any racist pretensions. There is no common system of measurement to compare and evaluate different ethnic groups. When one society tries to judge another, it applies its own criteria, and so commits intellectual violence. This same attitude can also be found in the crimes of globalization and Westernization, as well as in the American imperialism that makes them possible.

If we free socialism from its materialist, atheistic, and modernist features, and if we reject the racist and narrowly nationalist aspects of the Third Way, we arrive at a completely new kind of political ideology. We call it the Fourth Political Theory — the first being liberalism, which we are challenging; the second being the classical forms of Communism and socialism; and the third being fascism and National Socialism. The elaboration of the fourth begins at the point where the various anti-liberal political theories of the past intersect.

This brings us to National Bolshevism, which represents socialism without materialism, atheism, progressivism, and modernism, as well as the Third way without racism and nationalism. But this is only the first step. Merely revising the anti-liberal ideologies of the past doesn't give us the final result. It is only a first approximation and a preliminary approach. We should go further and appeal to Tradition and to pre-modern sources for inspiration. There we find the Platonic Ideals, the hierarchical societies of the medieval age, and theological visions of normative social and political systems, Christian, Islamic, Buddhist, Jewish, Hindu, or what have you. Pre-modernity is a very important source of the National Bolshevist synthesis. We need to find a new name for this kind of ideology, and "Fourth Political Theory" is quite appropriate for this. It doesn't tell us what this theory is, but rather what it isn't. Rather, it is a sort of invitation or appeal rather than a dogma.

Politically, this gives us an interesting foundation for conscious cooperation between Left wingers and Right wingers, as well as between religious or other anti-modern movements — the ecologists, for example. The only thing that we insist on in creating such an alliance is for those who participate to put aside their anti-Communist as well as anti-fascist prejudices. These prejudices are weapons in the hands of liberals and globalists with which they keep their enemies divided. We should strongly reject anti-Communism as well as anti-fascism. Both of them are counter-revolutionary tools in the hands of the global liberal elite. At the same time we should strongly oppose any kind of confrontation between religions: Muslims against Christians, Jews against Muslims, Muslims against Hindus, and so on. These interconfessional wars and hatreds work for the cause of the kingdom of Antichrist, which tries to divide all the traditional religions in order to impose its own pseudo-religion, the eschatological parody.

We need to unite the Right, the Left, and the traditional religions in a common struggle against the common enemy. Social justice, national sovereignty, and traditional values are the three primary principles of such an ideology. It is not easy to put all of this together, but we should try if we want to overcome the foe.

In French there is a slogan: *La droite des valeurs et la gauche du travail* (Alain Soral). In Italian it is, *La Destra sociale e la Sinistra identitaria*. How it should sound in English we will see later.

We could go further and try to define the subject, the actor of the Fourth Political Theory. In the case of Communism, class was at its center. In the case of the Third Way movements, the center was race or the nation. In the case of religions, it is the community of the faithful. How should the Fourth Political Theory deal with this diversity and this divergence of subjects? We propose, as a suggestion, that the subject of the Fourth Political Theory can be found in the Heideggerian concept of *Dasein* (being-t/here). It is a concrete but extremely profound notion that could be the common denominator for the further ontological development of this ideology. What is crucial here is the authenticity or non-authenticity of the existence of *Dasein*. The Fourth Political Theory insists on the authenticity of existence. Therefore, it is the antithesis to any kind of alienation — social, economic, national, religious, or metaphysical.

But *Dasein* is a concrete phenomenon. Any individual and any culture possesses its own *Dasein*. These manifestations differ between them, but they are always present.

If we accept that we should proceed to the elaboration of a common strategy in the pursuit of creating a future that will meet our demands and our vision, such values as social justice, national sovereignty, and traditional spirituality can serve as signposts along the way.

I sincerely believe that the Fourth Political Theory, National Bolshevism, and Eurasianism can be of great use to our peoples, our countries, and our civilizations. The key word is "multipolarity" in all senses — geopolitical, cultural, axiological, economic, and so on.

The important idea of *nous* (intellect) as defined by the Greek philosopher Plotinus corresponds to our ideal. The intellect is one and many at the same time, because it contains all kinds of differences within itself — not uniform or mixed, but taken as such with all their particularities. The future world should be noetic in some way — multiplicity and diversity should be understood as a wealth and as a treasure, and not as a reason for inevitable conflict. There should be many civilizations, many poles, many centers, and many sets of values on our one planet, and in our one humanity.

There are some who think otherwise. Who opposes such a project? Those who want to impose uniformity, one (American) way of life, and one world. They are doing it by force and by persuasion. They are against multipolarity. They are against us.

The Third Totalitarianism

A Critique from the Standpoint of the Fourth Political Theory

In political science, the concept of totalitarianism is held to be contained in both Communist and fascist ideologies, both of which openly proclaim the superiority of the whole (in Communism and socialism, class and society; in fascism, the state; and in National Socialism, race) over the private domain and the individual. To this they oppose the ideology of liberalism in which, on the contrary, the individual is placed above the whole, as if this whole could not be understood. As a consequence, liberalism combats totalitarianism in general, including that of Communism and fascism. Thus, the very term "totalitarianism" reveals its connection with liberal ideology — neither Communists nor fascists would see themselves in it. Everyone who uses the word "totalitarianism" is a liberal, whether they recognize it or not.

At first glance, this picture is perfectly clear and leaves no room for ambiguity: Communism is the first totalitarianism, and fascism is the second. Liberalism is its antithesis, as such denying the whole and putting the private above it. If we stop here, we will recognize that the modern era developed only two totalitarian ideologies: Communism (socialism) and fascism (National Socialism), along with their variations and nuances. But liberalism as a political theory appeared before the other two and outlasted them. It cannot therefore be called totalitarian. Hence the expression "third totalitarianism," which suggests that an expansion of the nomenclature of totalitarian ideologies, which includes liberalism, makes no sense.

However, the theme of the "third totalitarianism" may well appear in the context of classical French sociology (namely, the Durkheim school) and in postmodern philosophy. Durkheim's sociology maintains that the contents of individual consciousness are formed entirely on the basis of the collective consciousness. In other words, the "totalitarian" nature of any society, including individualistic and liberal types, cannot be changed. If the individual consciousness is derived from the collective, then the very act of declaring the individual as the highest value and measure of things as in liberalism is a projection of the society — that is, a form of totalitarian influence and of ideological conditioning. The notion of the individual is a social concept. A human being who exists outside of any society does not know whether or not he is an individual, or whether or not individualism is the highest value. The individual is taught that he is an individual only in a society where liberal ideology dominates and becomes an accepted, and therefore invisible, function of the social environment. Therefore, that which negates the social reality and affirms that of the individual is in itself of a social nature. Liberalism is a totalitarian ideology that insists, through the classic methods of totalitarian propaganda, that the individual has the highest value.

This is the beginning of a sociological critique of bourgeois society — not a socialist one, but one from a sociological standpoint (although often in France, and in the West more generally, socialism and sociology have converged almost to the point of merging into one another, as for example in Pierre Bourdieu's work). In this sense, the totalitarian character of liberalism is scientifically proven and the term "third totalitarianism" acquires logic and coherence, instead of being merely a shocking paradox. Toward this end one should take into consideration many of the concepts explored by sociology, such as the idea of the "lonely crowd" (*la foule solitaire*, as per David Riesman) as well as others.

Liberal society, which puts itself in opposition to the collective societies of socialism and fascism, has itself become a collective — a standardized and stereotypical one. The more an individual aspires to be unique within the context of the liberal paradigm, the more he becomes similar to everyone else. Liberalism brings with itself the stereotyping and homogenization of the world, which destroys all forms of diversity and differentiation.

On the other hand, there is postmodern philosophy. In the spirit of the search for radical immanence which is characteristic of the whole of modernity, postmodernists also raise the issue of the individual. According to them, individualism is synonymous with totalitarianism, but transposed to a micro level. The individual is a micro-totalitarianism that projects an apparatus of repression upon which social totalitarianism is built, at both the individualistic and sub-individualistic levels. In a Freudian spirit, viewing reason as an instrument for repression and alienation as well as a projection, postmodernists identify reason with the totalitarian state — that which suppresses its citizens' freedoms by imposing its point of view upon them. The individual is a concept that is a projection of the degradation and violence of a totalitarian society at its lowest levels. The desires and creative energies of the individual are continually obliterated. Above all, postmodernists believe that social totalitarianism (fascism and Communism) emerge out of the strict, hierarchical, and totalitarian structure of the rational individual. From this, the concept of liberal totalitarianism as a third totalitarianism derives its meaning and proves itself to be completely justified.

Hence, liberalism is a totalitarian and violent ideology — a means toward direct and indirect political repression, toward conditioning under pressure, and is a form of ferocious propaganda, which continually proclaims itself to be non-totalitarian; that is, it conceals its very nature. This is a scientific fact. The concept of the third totalitarianism is entirely consistent with liberalism's nature as a political concept.

The Fourth Political Theory accepts this concept completely, once the viewpoint that sees all three of the classical political theories of modernity (liberalism, Communism, and fascism) as being united is understood. All of them are totalitarian, although in different ways. The Fourth Political Theory likewise reveals the racist character of all three theories in a different context: the biological racism of the Nazis, Marx's class racism in his ideas concerning universal progress and evolution, and the civilizational, cultural, and colonial racism of the liberals. The latter was explicit until the mid-twentieth century and then became *sub rosa* after that (see John Hobson's *The Eurocentric Conception of World Politics*). The Fourth Political Theory rejects all types of totalitarianism — Communist, fascist or liberal. The third totalitarianism of today is the most dangerous one, since it is the ruling one. Fighting against it is a fundamental task.

The Fourth Political Theory proposes a completely new understanding of both the whole and its parts, outside the context of the three political ideologies of modernity. This understanding may be called an existential *Mit-sein*. But in this existential understanding of Being (*Dasein*), there is no atomized existence, meaning parts or individuals, nor a sum of individuals as in totalitarianism. In the Fourth Political Theory, living in association with others means to exist and constitutes Being — living in the face of death. We are together only when we are facing our own death. Death is always personal and, simultaneously, it is something common to us all. It is necessary for us not to talk about totalitarianism, which is merely a mechanical conception of how one should connect all the parts to the whole, but rather about an organic and existential holism. Its name is the People. *Dasein existiert völkisch.* In clear opposition to the third totalitarianism. For a Being-before-death. *Mit-sein.* We are the People.

Some Suggestions Regarding the Prospects for the Fourth Political Theory in Europe

To get to the Fourth Political Theory, we must begin from three ideological points.

From Liberalism to the Fourth Political Theory: The Hardest Road

To proceed from liberalism to the Fourth Political Theory is the most difficult path, since it is the opposite of all forms of liberalism. Liberalism is the essence of modernity, but the Fourth Political Theory considers modernity to be an absolute evil. Liberalism, which takes as its primary subject the individual and all the values and agendas that proceed from it, is viewed as the enemy. To embrace the Fourth Political Theory (4PT), a liberal should deny himself ideologically and reject liberalism and its suppositions in their entirety.

The liberal is an individualist. He is dangerous only when he is an extrovert, since in doing so he destroys his community and the social bonds with which he is associated. Being an introverted liberal is less dangerous because he only destroys himself, and this is a good thing: one liberal less.

But there is one interesting fact: the 4PT diverges from the modern versions of anti-liberalism (namely, socialism and fascism) by proposing not a critique of the individual as viewed from the outside, but rather his implosion. This means not to take a step back into pre-liberal forms of society, or one step sideways into the illiberal types of modernity, but rather one step inside the nihilistic nature of the individual as constructed by liberalism. Therefore, the liberal discovers his way to the 4PT when he takes one step further and achieves self-affirmation as the unique and ultimate instance of being. This is the final consequence of the most radical solipsism, and can lead to an implosion of the ego and the appearance of the real Self (which is also the goal of the practices associated with Advaita Vedanta).

Nietzsche called his *Übermensch* "the winner of God and nothing." By this he meant the overcoming of the old values of Tradition, but also the nothingness that comes in their place. Liberalism has accomplished the overcoming of God and the victory of pure nothingness. But this is the midnight before the breaking of dawn, so taking one step further into the midnight of European nihilism is how a liberal who wishes to leave this identity, which is more consistent with a peculiarly Western destiny of decline (because the Occident itself is nothing but decline at present — more on this later) behind, arrives at the horizon of the 4PT.

Modernity is certainly a European phenomenon. But liberalism as the essence of modernity is not so much European as Anglo-Saxon and trans-European, specifically North American. Europe was the preliminary stage of modernity, and thus Europe includes within itself the socialist (Communist) as well as fascist identities alongside the purely liberal one. Europe is the motherland of all three political theories. But America is a place where only one of them is deeply rooted and fully developed. Despite being born in Europe, liberalism has ripened in America. Europe and the US are comparable to father and child. The child inherited only one of the political possibilities from its father, albeit the most important one. As a result, liberalism in Europe is partly autochthonous and partly imposed by America (being re-exported). That is the reason why American followers of the 4PT are so important. If they manage to overcome liberalism in the Far West, they will show the path for European liberals to follow. This is something akin to Julius Evola's idea of differentiated man. This remark makes reference to my article about the 4PT in Europe and specifically to the final two propositions I make in it regarding how to overcome the individual: by method of self-transcendence by an effort of the will (a kind of polytheistic effort of pure will), or through an existential encounter with death and absolute loneliness.

Therefore, the way from liberalism to the 4PT in Europe passes through America and its inner mystics. This is the third attempt to make sense of America: the first one was that of de Tocqueville, the second was that of Jean Baudrillard. The third one is reserved for the European who approaches the Far West in a search for the mystery of liberalism from the 4PT perspective.

From Communism to the 4PT: From Radical Critics to the Principal Critics

The way from the Communist position to the 4PT is much easier and shorter. There are some common points: first of all, the radical rejection of liberalism, capitalism and individualism. There is a clear and definite common enemy. The problem is that the positive program of Communism is deeply rooted in modernity and shares many typically modern notions: the universality of social progress, linear time, materialistic science, atheism, Eurocentrism, and so on. The battle of Communism against capitalism belongs to the past. But the 4PT is the main ideological opponent of liberalism at present, so a genuine Communist can easily become attracted to the 4PT, considering its anti-liberal aspects.

To take this step, one needs to move on from the radical critics of modernity, such as Marx, to the principal critics of modernity, such as René Guénon, according to the excellent formulation of the French author, René Alleau. This brings us to the relevance of National Bolshevism. National Bolshevism is a kind of hermeneutics that identifies the qualitative features in the quantitative vision of socialism. For orthodox Marxists, society is based strictly on class principles and the socialist community is formed everywhere according to one model. But National Bolsheviks, having analyzed the Soviet, German and Chinese experiences, have remarked that, put into practice, Marxism can help to create societies with the clear features of a national culture and which possess specific and unique identities. While being theoretically internationalist, historical Communist societies were nationalist with strong traditional elements. Therefore socialism, being the by-product of liberal modernity, can be regarded as an extreme and heretical kind of pre-modernity and an eschatological form of ecstatic religiosity — following the examples of the Gnostics, the Cathars, Bruno, Müntzer, and so on. That was also the opinion of Eric Voegelin, who called this the immanentization of the eschaton. (This is a heretical notion, but it is traditional nevertheless.)

The way to the 4PT for the European Left passes through the historical and geopolitical analyses of the National Bolsheviks (Ernst Niekisch, Ernst Jünger and so on). Excellent work in this regard has been done by the European New Right and especially by Alain de Benoist.

From the Third Way to the 4PT: The Shortest Way but Problematic Nevertheless

From the European Third Way to the 4PT is only one step, because the 3PT and 4PT share the Conservative Revolution of the Weimar era and traditionalism as common starting points. But that step is not easy to take. The 4PT is strictly anti-modern, in fact counter-modern. The nation that is so dear to representatives of the Third Way is essentially a modern notion, just as are the concepts of the state and race. The 4PT is against any and all kinds of universalism, and refuses Eurocentrism of any kind — liberal as well as nationalist.

The ethnic traditions of the European peoples are sacred in their roots and form a part of their spiritual heritage. Yet ethnic identity is something quite different from the national state as a political body. European history was always based on the plurality of its cultures and the unity of its spiritual authorities. This was destroyed, first by the Protestant Reformation and then by modernity. The liquidation of European spiritual unity was part of the origin of European nationalism. Therefore the 4PT supports the idea of a new European empire as a traditional empire with a spiritual foundation, and with the dialectical coexistence of diverse ethic groups. Instead of national states in Europe, a sacred empire — Indo-European, Roman and Greek.

This is the dividing line between the European 4PT and the Third Way: the refusal of any kind of nationalism, chauvinism, Eurocentrism, universalism, racism, or xenophobic attitude. Historic pretensions and hostilities between the European ethnic groups existed, to be sure. It should be recognized. But it is irresponsible to construct a political program on that basis. Europe should stand for geopolitical unity, coupled with the preservation of the ethnic and cultural diversity of the various European ethnoses.

The 4PT affirms that geopolitics is the primary instrument that can be used to understand the contemporary world, so Europe should be reconstructed as an independent geopolitical power. All these points coincide with the main principles of the French New Right and with the manifesto of GRECE by Alain de Benoist (*Manifesto for a European Renaissance* [London: Arktos, 2011]). Therefore we should consider the European New Right as a manifestation of the 4PT.

Here we approach the philosophy of Martin Heidegger, who is central to and the most important thinker for the 4PT. The 4PT takes as its primary subject the Heideggerian notion of *Dasein*. Heidegger is the metaphysical (fundamental-ontological) step from the Third Way toward the Fourth one. The task is to develop the implicit political philosophy of Heidegger into an explicit one, thus creating as a consequence a doctrine of existential politics.

Last point. Europe is the West, and decline is its essence. To come to the lowest point of its descent (*Niedergang*) is the fate of Europe. It is deeply tragic, and not something one should be proud of. The 4PT is in favor of a European Idea in which Europe is understood as a sort of tragic community (as per Georges Bataille): a culture that is searching for itself in the heart of Hell.

The Fourth Political Theory in America

Some Suggestions for the American People

People as Existence

The Fourth Political Theory refuses the three major forms of political modernity: liberalism (the first political theory), Communism/socialism (the second) and fascism/National Socialism (the third). The 4PT considers itself as essentially non-modern or counter-modern. This signifies that it could be considered pre-modern as well as postmodern (this is another postmodernity — not purely deconstructive but also re-constructive).

The three main political theories of modernity each deal with a central subject. The subject of liberalism is the individual; that of Communism is class (or rather two antagonist classes); that of fascism is the national state or race (as in National Socialism).The 4PT suggests a quite different subject — a fourth subject. It can be identified as the concept of the people (in its simple, political version) and as Heideggerian *Dasein* (in its philosophical version). Alain de Benoist prefers people. I myself am inclined toward *Dasein*. But the sense of the two terms in the semantic context of the 4PT is not so divergent. The concept of the people in the 4PT is conceived as an existential category. The people is existence. Heidegger said: *Dasein existiert völkisch* (Being t/here exists as people, through people). To be, for concrete human beings, means first of all to be German, French, Russian, American, Chinese, African, and so on. Without this identity the human is deprived of language, culture, mentality, traditions, social status and roles. The people is the reality closest to the very essence of man. Thinking, acting, willing, creating, and fighting as a person means one always thinks, acts, desires, creates, and fights as a German, French, Russian, American, Chinese, African and so on.

The concept of people in the 4PT is not a formal and explicit category like that of the nation, but an informal and implicit category that lies beneath any concretization. The 4PT is dealing with people and regards the world as a multiplicity of peoples, each one of them representing a particular and incommensurable horizon of being.

Such an approach evokes the problem of identity that is at the center of the 4PT.

Three Kinds of Identity

In order to clarify the 4PT let us delve into the problem of identity. We propose a methodological schema. We can represent the identity of a certain society or community as having three dimensions:

1. Diffused identity. This is a vague feeling of a common belonging to a certain whole that is proper to every member of a given society. It is somehow confused, uncertain, unconscious and weak. It can be activated only in an extreme situation such as wars, revolutions, natural disasters, and so on. Diffused identity doesn't make a direct impact on political or ideological decisions or choices. People with the same diffused identity can freely choose quite different methods, values, solutions, and strategies, can belong to different and concurrent parties, can share different positions on concrete issues, and so on. Such identity is weak, unconscious, and in times of peace almost nonexistent, because it doesn't affect the person in his everyday life.

2. Extreme identity. This is an arbitrary and artificial creation of some rational formula that pretends to express and manifest the diffused identity in the intellectual realm. Here the identity becomes an ideology, a conceptual framework, or a theory. An example of such an identity is nationalism. But there can be other types, such as social or class identities, liberal cosmopolite identity, and so on. It tries to convince the bearers of diffused identity that this represents their essence. It is not so popular in times of peace and prosperity but usually gains popularity in periods of wars and troubles. Extreme identity is often a perverted, disfigured, and exotic creation that contrasts with the diffused identity, emphasizing certain features and neglecting oth-

ers. Extreme identity is often the caricature of diffused identity. This identity is much clearer and conscious and influences formal decisions, allegiances, solutions, and options for the people who accept and cultivate it.

3. Deep identity. The third type of identity is the privileged one in the 4PT. Deep identity is an organic, existential, basic identity that lies below diffused identity, giving it its content, meaning and structure. It is a kind of language (in the structuralist context of Ferdinand de Saussure) that contains all kinds of possible discourses. It is not a superstructure that is constructed above diffused identity (as extreme identity) but an infrastructure that is beneath diffused identity, giving it reality, sense, and inner harmony. Deep identity is what causes a people to be what it is. It is the essence of the people, something that transcends the collectivity in its actual state. This is transcendence: people being simultaneously immanent and present in every other person that belongs to the same people. The people is not what exists at the present time. Its language, culture, tradition, gestures, and psychological features don't appear in the present, they come from the past and move toward the future through the present moment. An actually existing people is not a people as such but only a particular moment of it, and only a segment of it. The people includes those who are dead and those of its children who have yet to be born. It is a kind of music that can be perceived as such only if we remember the previous note and anticipate the next one. The deep identity is the whole that plays out in both time and space. Deep identity is people as existence.

The 4PT is dealing with people as existence, and therefore the question of the deep identity of each people is of primordial importance.

American deep identity

In thinking of how to apply the 4PT in the United States, we first need to find its subject, to discover deep identity there, and to affirm the American people as existing. Here we immediately come across some serious problems. The US was founded as a purely conceptual society conveying the very essence of modernity. Modern anthropology is based on equating humanity with the individual. The individual is a concept constructed out of an atomistic vision of nature and society. The individual is a social atom. But we know now that in modern physics, more and more sub-atomic structures are being discovered. The meanings of the words *a-tom* (Greek) and *individual* (Latin) are precisely "what cannot be further divided." But there is no such entity in nature. It is no more than a concept. Natural science thus continues to search for more and more sub-atomic levels. The social sciences of modernity have stopped at the level of the individual, operating with this concept as the central point of all the sciences. Socialist doctrines tried to think in terms of the social systems of individuals. Postmodern theories delve into sub-individual spheres. But modernity deals with man in terms of individual anthropology. In liberalism it became the core of its political, economic, and juridical theory.

Likewise, American society was constructed on the basis of this concept. It is a very individualistic society and very liberal in all senses. It is strictly coeval with European modernity. It was born modern. This is important. To be born modern means that the US never *became* modern; it has never been pre-modern. It is not relatively modern. It is absolutely modern. The US doesn't know what it is like to be unmodern. The pre-modern tribes of American Indians were completely annihilated by the European settlers, many of them during the Revolutionary War (the majority of the Indians fought on the side of the British). For European people, modernity was an epoch that developed only after the pre-modern Middle Ages; therefore the roots of the European people are pre-modern. That is their past and their semantic prelude to modernity. Modernity is the negation of pre-modernity: secularism against theocracy, the nation-state against empire, the human against the divine, and the individual against the state, *ethos*, religious community, and so on. Positive modern values were constructed upon the denial of superseded, obsolete pre-modern values.

America completely lacks pre-modernity. It has never been an empire, theocracy, or caste society. As a result it is missing such deep dimensions. This is a difference between the US and Latin America. Latin America was never cut off so radically from Mother Europe. It was conceived as a peripheral part of Europe, and maintained strong ties to her. Latin America was part of European history, and so it has inherited European pre-modernity — Catholicism, the idea of empire, caste society, and so on. Modernity for Latin America has the same sense as it has for Europe: it is one step beyond its pre-modern roots. So South America is much more European than America, and its deep identity is much easier to discover. Its roots are Latin: Spanish, Portuguese, Catholic, and Mediterranean.

The only root of American society is the modern concept of the individual. There is nothing that lies beneath the individual. There is no pre-modern dimension to it and no deep roots. America came into existence too late to have genuine rootedness in its soil.

This poses a real problem in the search for deep identity there, and thus makes the application of the 4PT in American society difficult.

The soil that lacks

The question of roots in the search for deep identity evokes the concepts of soil, space, and of landscape. The people live in a space. Heidegger wrote, "*Dasein existiert räumlich.*" *Dasein* exists as space and through space. A people exists through space. The landscape is the living image of the country and the people that dwells there. The soil is sacred for deep identity as the most basic, vegetative level of the soul. The soil of Europe is a kind of visible, material manifestation of its culture. The German archaeologist and anthropologist Leo Frobenius used to say, "Culture is the Earth manifesting itself through man."

Deep identity is linked to the soil. It is the dimension of eternity, of everlasting stability and immutability.

America has no soil, or rather, the soil that it has doesn't belong to Americans. The soil is essentially pre-modern. American society was constructed while completely neglecting the soil. The real living space belongs to those who inhabited the continent before the Whites, to the Indian. To them, the soil does matter. It is the basis of the Indian soul. This was not the case with the White settlers. They settled in the middle of nowhere in order to create a utopia, a place that cannot exist in space. From the beginning, America was a mobile, highly dynamic society of nomads moving about on the surface of a minimized, almost non-existent space. There is no such thing as American earth. There is no earth there, there is only America, the country without soil, without roots, open to all and allowing no one a place to exist — only a place to keep moving, endlessly and always, developing, progressing, and changing. It is a pure dromocratic society[1] (Paul Virilio), a suc-

---

1   Virilio coined the term "dromocratic" to describe what he saw as the most salient feature of modernity, which is the pursuit of ever-increasing speed through technical and scientific advancement. Virilio believed that we are approaching the limit of such speed, and that the reaching of this limit would mean the end of modernity.

cessfully realized rhizomatic smooth surface,[2] as was dear to Gilles Deleuze.

Therefore, the space of America doesn't allow roots to grow. It is an asphalt world. The space of America was virtual from the very beginning of its civilization. The invention of cyberspace was only a delayed iteration of this reality that was achieved long ago.

Negri and Hardt, who see in the US the clearest example of postmodernity as the achievement of the most purified form of modernity, are quite right. The American Empire is deeply postmodern. Its only root is modernity, so it is free to grow without roots — without space in the middle of an entirely artificial landscape, under an electric sky.

The absence of soil is a dramatic obstacle in the search for deep identity. This prevents the projection of the 4PT onto American society. We need to resolve this problem somehow. By accepting that the very structure of American society is missing the profound dimension of existential depth that is present in all other cultures and civilizations, we can nevertheless suggest some paths to explore.

The liberalism that is at the heart of American society and the individualism that forms its core values should be accepted as basic features of American identity. That is the birthmark of the artificial construction of American society as a laboratory project of Western modernity.

Liberalism and individualism represent the two main characteristics of diffused identity. To be American means to be liberal, individualistic, progressive, and modern. It is not a fixed state, it is a process. The US is not being but becoming. Above this diffused identity there are two parallel mainstream ideological narratives: Democrat and Republican. They are the summary of diffused identity, conveying and deforming it simultaneously in their rational approximations. Liberalism is the center — Democrats are a little to the Left, Republicans a little to the Right. But both these forms of external identity are based on consensus. All other proposals for the formulation of a new political identity are marginalized because there is insufficient social support for such alternative formulations. The American bipartite political-ideological structure is almost a mathematical expression of the American identity, oscillating around its main vectors — liberalism, individualism, freedom, progress, process, development, efficiency, and so on.

---

2   To Deleuze, a smooth space was any sociological realm that allows its inhabitants to move about free of obstruction, as opposed to a "striated space," which is partitioned and prevent easy movement.

Under such conditions there is no deep dimension. Asphalt and the smooth virtual surface don't allow depth to exist. America is a very shallow, hollow society. Its superficiality is the reason for its troubles, but also for its victories.

When viewed in its normal state, we arrive at the conclusion that there cannot be deep identity there, because Americans lack soil, a pre-modern legacy, depth, and roots. Therefore the 4PT is closed to Americans. It seems that this is true for the majority, who are fully satisfied with the status quo. At the same time, however, existence in the Heideggerian sense presupposes awareness of being t/here. To live without roots means to turn to ritual and to depersonalize oneself. To be content with conceptual individualism and possessing no ground for one's being is the same as agreeing to a purely mechanical form of existence: to become a machine, not human. Without depth there is no existence, so there can be no human being. This is the reason why the 4PT is very important to the US. It is the only way to save its human core as it undergoes the process of total dehumanization, mechanization and postmodern transhumanization. The 4PT is the destiny of the human beings of America, not of individualistic robots.

In dealing with American society we need to keep in mind that we are dealing with organic liberals and individualists. We cannot change it. We need to accept it and try to install an existential politics within the core of such a unique and particular society. The people is the whole that is more than the sum of its parts. The American people are the parts that think that they are whole in themselves, and that there is no need for any other whole. Americans are parts without the whole. This might seem strange, but it is so.

Americans are liberal and individualist. This is a real challenge for the 4PT. How do we solve this difficult equation?

European soil

There are three solutions to the existential problem of America's lack of soil.

The first one is obvious. It is an invitation to discard one's American identity and pass on to another existential camp. The simplest way to do this is to return to one's European roots. This means that the American stops considering himself as being an American, and begins to regard his situation in the light of Mother Europe. Thus the American becomes European anew, but a European who happens to be located outside of Europe. This renders the US as the New World no longer, but rather the Western periphery of the Old World. To be American is the same as to be a European in exile. One can recall one's ancestors and revive one's national or ethnic, as well as the religious identity of one's European forefathers. One becomes German-American, Italian-American, Russian-American, Polish-American, and so on. In this way, one can freely choose their European identity. For example Eugene (Seraphim) Rose, who was of purely Anglo-Saxon descent, converted to Orthodoxy and has nearly become a Russian Orthodox saint. He fully accepted the traditional Russian identity. The other example is the greatest American poet, Ezra Pound, who identified with European culture and who lived for many years in Europe, and who stood on the side of the Central European powers against the US. It is actually quite simple for an American to take such a step to re-actualize or artificially create a European cultural and intellectual Self.

This step immediately changes one's existential horizons. In obtaining a European identity the ex-American receives the most important existential dimensions: roots, soil, and history. He obtains depth. That is most important. In Heideggerian terms it means the re-acquisition of the History of Being, *Seynsgeschichte*. The individual is situated both in the European space (on its periphery) and in the flow of European time. He immediately receives a pre-modern basis for his own existence. He becomes the bearer of European destiny and a part of the European *logos*.

This option assimilates the ex-American with other Europeans, and in this case the 4PT is based on the Heideggerian concept of *Dasein*, *Ereignis* and the Last God.[3] The deep identity of Europe is in its being the West, the dark side of ontology, and the place of Descent (*Niedergang*). Europe is the space of the final tragedy, or Ragnarok, the final battle of the gods.

Europe is the place where the eschatology of Being is consumed: the point of the Turn (*Kehre*). 4PT in this case is quite clear: it is the invitation to destroy modernity, resolving its nihilistic enigma and passing to a new beginning. The individual, the class, and the nation (race) are all artificial constructions of the perverted and nihilistic metaphysics of the Enlightenment. They are forms of inauthentic existence, for they mislead the real Self of being t/here and promote the totalitarian dictatorship of liberalism, one way or another, and of impersonal mechanical power.

---

3   Heidegger believed that the Last God would re-emerge once Western man proceeded beyond the rationalist metaphysics that has dominated his thought in recent centuries, and would allow him to reconnect with an authentic mode of Being.

Therefore, the 4PT for European-Americans is just the same as for native Europeans. The fact that the European-American is oriented more toward the West, indeed the far West, adds eschatological tension to this existential awakening of authentic *Dasein*. Heidegger is the destiny of European America, and its most important author.

In this case all periods of Heidegger are equally valuable, especially his early texts: *Being and Time* as well as *Contributions to Philosophy*, and his other writings on the History of Being.

Heavenly Soil

The second suggestion is much harder. It demands some philosophical explications.

Let us take the purely liberal, individualist American. His diffused identity has formed him entirely and he has no inclination to become European. He wants to remain American. But he asks about his deep identity. He isn't satisfied by the proposed bipartite model, has been deceived by many marginal alternatives, and cannot accept the mechanical lifestyle that he shares with the American majority — the innocence of ultimate idiocy. He tries to discover depth, but there is no such dimension in America. All is covered by asphalt. No roots, no nature, no past. The artificiality of the everlasting present is omnipresent. Such a man needs soil. He asks about the reason for his existence, but he can find no answer. What is there to do?

In such circumstances one can try to repeat the Cartesian experience. There is an ego, an individual that thinks. This ego is here and is present. There is no past in this society, only an ephemeral moment. There is no ground beneath. But the man exists, so there should be a ground and soil. He couldn't spring out of the asphalt. Now he decides: if there is no soil under me, there should be soil over me. It is the Heavenly Earth[4] (Henry Corbin) imagined or rationally discovered by the individual. American culture demands that a person should conceive of himself as an individual, so in being an American and in thinking about the direct cause and reason for one's own existence, one arrives at the concept of the Heavenly Motherland

---

4   For Corbin, the Heavenly Earth is the imaginal realm in which ideas are apprehended in their essence through spiritual disciplines and investigations, similar to the realm of Ideas that lies behind the world of the senses that Plato discussed.

and of an individual god (or individual spirit) that is responsible for the existence of this person. Mainstream culture doesn't talk about such things, but since one is allowed to think freely it is quite logical for him to do so. Every individual should discover this god and this heavenly soil for himself. This is the rule in American society. If he doesn't seek such causes, he could be free in his ignorance. But if he does seek it he should arrive at the answer for himself.

We are coming to a very important conclusion: there is a premise for a very special American form of theology, an inverted individualist Platonism that discovers the transcendence of God by creating it for himself.

American theology is comparable to rain — each drop is the American soul created by the American rain, which is a rain of spirit. Such a theology is individually monotheistic, socially polytheistic (there are many drops of rain), and normatively secular or atheistic. Each person can discover his or her personal god or spirit. Such an occasion is pragmatically necessary for everyone. But it cannot be imposed from the outside. It should be sought and found starting from the inside.

The individual god/spirit creates the individual, but does not determine him forever. That would mean that change is impossible. But American diffused identity is based on change. American theology should therefore be a process theology. The multiplicity of strictly individual gods/spirits are creating and recreating Americans always anew. American individuality is becoming, and dynamic. It is open individuality, not horizontally but vertically. The US is a community of deeply individualistic mystics. This can't be proved but it can't be denied nonetheless. It represents an American secret. You can assume that you are dealing with a fool, but maybe he is a fool of god (or spirit).

American theology presents a new version of the deep dimension. The 4PT in such a case addresses not the superficial side of the American mentality (the purely mechanical one), but speaks directly to this secret side of the American personality: its dimension of spirit-rain. The American exists by creating his personal god for himself. It is a rain that is falling upwards rather than down. This voluntary transcendence serves as a depth that can and should arise out of the banality of the ideology of modernity. It is a kind of secret side of liberalism where its limitations are transcended out of the heroic efforts of absolute loneliness. The US is the only place where such absolute loneliness is possible. To transcend that is obligatory.

A person, in the process of creating his creator, thus installs the dimension of depth into his personal anthropology. Imagining the past and history is certainly a possible target for the 4PT. Such an effort is too dramatic for modernity. Therefore individuality is brought and imposed by modernity. But the American who lives in such conditions, and who tries to grasp the cause and meaning of his existence in America (America isn't the world — so Heideggerian existentialism should be corrected here to in-America-being, in-America-*sein*) provokes self-implosion. He tragically realizes the absent vertical axis in himself and is then ready to receive the 4PT.

American way of death

The last path toward deep identity in American society is that of classical American existentialism as represented in American literature and art. In this case it is that of a lonely individual losing his usual way of life and leaving the closed circle of mean-ingless dynamism that is America. The American is rejected by America. Now he is in trouble. There is no way out of America. If you can't find a way to be part of America, you will pay for it. Being in America is fateful. Society gives you only one thing — an absolute individual freedom, but confiscates all others. You are free from everything. At the same time you are free for nothing. Therefore an outsider discovers himself, by himself. But America is the universal outsider. To find your-self outside of the camp of being and to live in America are the same thing. Those who understand that are more American than those who don't. The real American is the lost American, the confused American, the fallen American...

Seeking for the soil in such a situation leads, as we have already seen, to no-where. There is no soil, no roots, and no past. The American can only slide across the smooth surface of the eternal present. And if one falls, he continues to exist sliding — falling, fallen. There are cases when the individual cannot look upward in the direction of the Heavenly Earth. Not a drop of rain. There is no will or strength to create a personal god/spirit. That leaves only one option — death. In America, death is individualistic. It is antisocial. It doesn't concern anybody ex-cept he who is dying. All those who have gone astray begin to be-in-front-of-death, without hope or sense. This is pure, liberal death and the essence of liberty. The heroes of J. D. Salinger, John Updike, William Faulkner, or the beatniks are exam-ples of such types of American outsiders who are actually the only genuine insiders, because they have arrived at the core of the American identity, which is death itself.

The 4PT is based on a *Dasein* that exists authentically. This means that we exist before death, looking straight into her eyes. This is the needed dimension. In confronting death we awaken the content of our being. We are not always human, but we become such when we realize our mortality and finite nature. When our end is before us, that is a moment for beginning. American outsiders are ready subjects for the 4PT. They discover the nucleus of liberalism and the center of individuality — it is death. But death, descent, *Niedergang* should be taken as a starting point for the 4PT. The death of the subject of all the classical political theories of modernity is the birth of real *Dasein* and its manifestation.

Three paths for America

We have made a survey of three ways to discover the deep identity of the American people. The first is an invitation to abdicate one's modern, American identity and return to the European one. In this case the American people is considered as an extension of the European people.

The second one suggests affirming a special American theology, or rain-spirit, with an artificially created transcendence that would prepare a new concept for the American people as mystical individualists creating gods/spirits. Some examples of this type of identity can be seen in various American religious sects: the Mormons, the Process Church[5] and Process theology, the many diverse Protestant denominations, and so on. Here we see the implosion of modernity that prepares the route for the acceptance of the counter-modern essence of the 4PT.

The third method is the direct confrontation with death and the discovery of the nothingness that lies at the center of the individual as such. The nihilistic essence of liberalism here becomes evident, and starting from this black spot we can further consider the propositions of the 4PT on how to overcome it.

---

5   The Process Church of the Final Judgment was established in London, and later New Orleans, during the 1960s and '70s. Based on Christian theology, it taught that the opposition of Christ and Satan in fact formed a unity, and that the divine beings exist within every individual.

GLOBAL REVOLUTION

The Manifesto of the Global Revolutionary Alliance

Program, Principles, Strategy

Dissatisfied all over the world, unite!

Part One: The Situation of the End

1. *We live at the end of the historical cycle.* All processes that constitute the flow of history have come to a logical impasse.

   a. *The end of capitalism.* The development of capitalism has reached its natural limit. There is only one path left to the world economic system — to collapse in upon itself. Based on a progressive increase in the purely financial institutions — first banks, and then more complex and sophisticated stock structures — the system of modern capitalism has become completely divorced from reality, from the balance of supply and demand, from the production and consumption ratio, and from a connection with real life. All the wealth of the world is concentrated in the hands of the world's financial oligarchy by means of complex manipulations of artificial financial pyramids. This oligarchy has devalued not only labor, but also the capital connected to the market fundamentals, which has been secured through financial rent. All other economic forces are held in bondage to this impersonal, transnational, ultra-liberal elite. Regardless of how we feel about capitalism, it is clear now that it is not just going through another crisis, but that the entire system stands on the verge of total collapse. No matter how the global oligarchy tries to conceal the ongoing collapse from the masses of the world's population, more and more people are beginning to suspect that this is inevitable, and that the global financial crisis, which was caused by the collapse of the American mortgage market and its major banks, is only the beginning of a global catastrophe. This catastrophe can be delayed, but it cannot be prevented or avoided. The world economy, in the form in which it now operates, is doomed.

b. *The end of resources.* In the current demographic situation, taking into account the steady growth of the world's population, especially in the countries of the Third World, humanity has come close to exhausting the Earth's natural resources. These are necessary not just to maintain our current levels of consumption, but for sheer survival at even a minimal level. We are fast approaching the limits of economic growth, and global hunger, deprivation, and epidemics will become the new norm. We have exceeded the carrying capacity of the Earth. Hence, we face an imminent demographic catastrophe. The more children who are born, the greater the suffering will ultimately be. This problem has no easy solution, but to pretend that it doesn't exist is to walk blind into the worst-case scenario of our global collective suicide as a species at the hands of our own economic system and its uncontrolled growth.

c. *The end of society.* Under the influence of Western and American values, the atomization of the world's societies, in which people are no longer connected with each other by any form of social bonds, is in full swing. Cosmopolitanism and a new nomadism has become the most common lifestyle, especially for the younger generation. This, coupled with economic instability and environmental catastrophe, provokes unprecedented streams of emigrants, which is destroying entire societies. Cultural, national, and religious ties are being broken, social contracts are being broken, and organic connections are being severed. We live in a world of lonely crowds — societies atomized by the cult of individualism. Cosmopolitan loneliness is becoming the norm and cultural identities are imploding. Societies are being replaced by nomadism and the coldness of the Internet, which dissolve organic, historical collectives. At the same time culture, language, morality, tradition, values, and the family as an institution are disappearing.

d. *The end of the individual.* The division of the individual into his component parts is becoming the dominant trend. Human identities are spread across virtual networks, assuming online personas and turning into a game of disorganized elements. Paradoxically, when one abandons his integrity, he is granted more freedoms, but at the cost of someone — his lost self — who could make better use of them. Postmodern culture compulsively exports people to virtual worlds of electronic screens and removes them from reality, capturing them in a flow of subtly organized and cleverly manipulated hallucinations. These processes are managed by the global oligarchy, which seeks to make the world's masses complacent, controllable and programmable. Never before has individualism been glorified so much, yet at the same time, never before have people all over the world been so similar to each other in their behavior, habits, appearance, techniques, and tastes. In the pursuit of individualistic "human rights" humanity has lost itself. Soon man will be replaced by the post-human: a mutant, cloned android.

e. *The end of nations and peoples.* Globalization and global governance interfere in the domestic affairs of sovereign states, erasing them one by one, and systematically destroy all national identity. The global oligarchy seeks to dissolve all national borders that might impede its ubiquitous presence. Transnational corporations put their own interests above national interests and state administrations, which leads to a state's dependence on systems outside of itself, and the loss of its independence to be replaced by interdependence. The system of international relations is being supplanted by the structures of the global financial oligarchy. Western countries and monopolies form the core of this global governance, and they are gradually integrating the economic and political elites of the non-Western states as well. Thus, the former national elites have become accomplices of the processes of globalization, betraying the interests of their states and of their fellow citizens, forming a global transnational class in which they have more in common with each other than with their former countrymen.

f. *The end of knowledge.* The global mass media creates a system of total disinformation, organized in accordance with the interests of the global oligarchy. Only that which is reported by the global media constitutes "reality." The word of the global Fourth Estate becomes a "self-evident truth," otherwise known as "conventional wisdom." Alternative viewpoints can still be spread through the interstices of the global communication networks, but they are condemned to the margins because financial support is provided only for those informational outlets that serve the interests of the global oligarchy, or in other words, capital. When critical opinions pass a certain threshold and become a threat to the system, the classical instruments of repression are called upon: financial pressure, deprication, demonization, and legal and physical harassment. In such a society, the entire system through which knowledge of all types is disseminated becomes something universally moderated by this global, transnational media elite.

g. *The end of progress.* In recent centuries, humanity has lived by faith in progress and in hope for a better future. This promise was seen in the development of the positivist methodology, breakthroughs in knowledge and science, and the appearance and evolution of the notions of humanism and social justice. Progress seemed to be guaranteed and self-evident. In the twenty-first century this belief is shared only by the naïve, who deliberately turn a blind eye to reality in order to be rewarded with a life of material privilege and peace of mind. But this belief in progress refutes itself. Both the individual and the world are not getting better, but, on the contrary, are rapidly degenerating — or, at the very least, they remain just as cruel, cynical and unfair as ever. The discovery of this fact has led to the collapse of the humanistic worldview. Only the consciously blind choose not to see that, under the double standards of the Western world and its catchy slogans about human rights and freedom, lies an egoistic will to colonize and control. Progress is not only not guaranteed, but unlikely. If things continue to develop as they are today, the most pessimistic, catastrophic, and apocalyptic prognoses of the future will come to pass.

2. In general, *we are dealing with the end of a vast historical cycle,* whose basic parameters are exhausted and upset. The expectations that had been a part of it are being erased or have proven to be deceptions. The end of the world does not simply happen, it unfolds before our eyes. We are both observers and participants in the process. Does it herald the end of modern civilization or the end of mankind? No one can predict with certainty. But the scale of the disaster is such that we cannot rule out the possibility that the agonizing death-throes of the globalist, Western-centric world will drag all of us into the abyss with it. The situation is becoming even more dramatic by virtue of the fact that, under the existing institutions of global governance and international finance by which the transnational oligarchy dictates its will

to the world, these catastrophic processes cannot continue as before since their threshold has been reached. The growing crisis cannot be stopped even as they are propelled by their own inertia, nor can their course be changed since the rapid pace of such major trends doesn't allow for an abrupt course-change to modify its trajectory.

3. *The current situation is intolerable*, not only as it is, but also because of where it is going. *Today, a catastrophe; tomorrow, species-wide suicide.* Mankind has stolen its future from itself. But man differs from animals by having an understanding of history. Even if at a given moment one doesn't feel all the exigencies of the situation, one's knowledge of the past and foresight of a manufactured future reproduces both optimistic and ominous perspectives — the utopian and the dystopian. Seeing the path we have already tread over our shoulder, and looking down the path ahead, we cannot afford to misjudge or fail to notice that the path we are on leads to our doom. Only those who are deprived of historical thought, reduced to an existence as "consumers" by an unending and aggressive flow of advertising, mindless entertainment, and disinformation, and who are cut off from genuine education and culture, can ignore the horror of our actual situation. Only a brute or a consuming automaton — the posthuman — can fail to recognize the world for the catastrophe it has become.

4. Those that have saved at least a grain of independent and free intellect can't help but wonder: what is the *reason* for our current situation? What are the origins and triggers of this disaster? It is now clear that the cause is Western civilization — its technological development, individualism, its pursuit of freedom at any cost, materialism, economic reductionism, egoism, and a fetish for money — that is , essentially the whole of bourgeois-capitalist liberal ideology. The cause also lies in the racist belief of Western societies that their values and beliefs are universal, and are the best ones and therefore obligatory for the rest of humanity. If at first this passion yielded positive results — engendering new dynamics, opening up possibilities for humanism, creating an extended zone of freedom, an improved material situation for some, and the opening of new perspectives — then after reaching its limit the same trends began producing the opposite results. The technique turned from an instrument into a self-sufficient principle (the prospect for mechanized revolt); individualism carried to extremes, being deprived of one's own

nature, freedom losing its subject, the idolatry of the material leading to spiritual degradation, society destroyed by egoism, the absolute power of money exploiting labor and exorcising the entrepreneurial spirit of capitalism, and liberal ideology destroying any form of social, cultural or religious solidarity. In the West this course grew out of the logic of their historical development, but in the rest of the world, the same principles were imposed by force through colonial and imperialist practices, without taking into account the specificities of local cultures. The West, having embarked on this path in the modern era, not only brought itself to a lamentable ending, but also caused irreparable damage to all the other nations on the Earth. It is *not* universal, in the true meaning of the word, but it and its catastrophic course have been *made* universal and global, such that it is no longer possible to separate or isolate oneself from it. The only change possible is to uproot, root and branch, the entire system and its paradigm. And despite the fact that in non-Western societies the situation is somewhat different, simply ignoring the challenge of the West cannot change anything. The roots of the evil have run too deep. They should be clearly understood, comprehended, identified, and put in the spotlight. One cannot fight consequences without understanding their causes.

5.   Just as there are causes for the current disastrous situation, likewise there are those whose interests depend on the status quo — who want it to last, profit from it, are responsible for it, support it, strengthen it, and protect and guard it, as well as prevent it from changing its course of development. This is the global oligarchic transnational class, which includes the political, financial, economic, and military-strategic core of the world's elite (mostly Western), as well as a broad network of intellectuals who serve it, and executives and media moguls who form their loyal entourage. Taken together, the global oligarchy and its attendants are the ruling class of globalism. It includes political leaders of the United States, economic and financial moguls, and the agents of globalization who serve them and make up the gigantic planetary network in which resources are allocated to those who are loyal to the thrust of globalization. They also direct the flow of information; control political, cultural, intellectual, and ideological lobbying; perform data collection; and infiltrate the structures of those states which have not yet been fully deprived of their sovereignty, not to mention their use of outright corrup-

tion, bribery, influence, harassment of dissenters, and so on. This globalist network consists of multiple levels, including both political and diplomatic missions, as well as multinational corporations and their management, media networks, global trade and industry structures, non-governmental organizations and funds, and the like. The catastrophe in which we all find ourselves, and which is coming to its head, is entirely man-made. There are forces that will do anything to maintain the status quo. They are the architects and managers of the global, egocentric, hyper-capitalistic world. They are responsible for everything. Global oligarchy and its network of agents is the root of all evil. Evil is personified in the global political class. The world is as it is because someone wants it to be like this, and puts a great deal of effort into making it so. This drive is the quintessence of this historical evil. But if this is indeed the case, and someone is responsible for the present situation, then the opposition and dissenting from the status quo obtains its target. Global oligarchy becomes the enemy of all mankind. But the very presence of an identifiable enemy gives us a chance to defeat them, a chance for salvation, and an opportunity to overcome the catastrophe.

Part Two: The Image of a Normal World

We are told, through attempted hypnosis and propaganda, that things cannot be any other way than they are now, and that any alternative would be even worse. This familiar tune tells us that "democracy has many flaws, but all other political regimes are so much worse, that it is better to accept what we already have." This is a falsehood and political propaganda. The world we live in is unacceptable, intolerable, and leading to our inevitable civilizational suicide. Finding an alternative to it is necessary for survival. If we don't overthrow the status quo, don't change the course of the development of civilization, don't deprive of power and destroy the global oligarchy as a system and as manipulative forces, groups, institutions, corporations and even individuals, we'll become not only victims but also complicit in the impending end. The claim that "everything is not so bad," that "it was worse before," that "somehow everything will get better," and so on, is a deliberate form of hypnotic suggestion that is intended to lull the remnants of free consciousness and independent and sober analysis into apathy. The global oligarchy cannot allow their underlings to dare to think independently and outside of the framework of their secretly imposed standards. This elite does not act directly, as in the totalitarian regimes of the past, but subtly and insidiously, making people take their dogmas for granted and even making them seem as if they are freely adopted by each person. But human dignity depends on the ability to choose between saying "yes" or "no" to the current situation. No entity can force a "yes" from a person and have it be a humane "yes." One can say "no" to anything, at any time and under any circumstances. In denying this basic right, the global elite denies us our human dignity. That means it opposes not only humanity, but humaneness and human nature. This alone gives us the right to revolt against it, to radically say "no" to it and to the whole state of affairs, to refute its suggestions, to awaken from its hypnosis, and to instead imagine another world, another way, a different order, a different system, and a different present and future. The world that surrounds us is unacceptable. It is bad from any point of view. It is unjust, disastrous, untrustworthy, and deceitful. It is not free. It must be crushed and destroyed. We need a different world. It will not be worse, as the global oligarchy and its loyal servants tell us in an attempt to frighten us. It will be better and it will be the path to salvation.

What is, in this case, a better world, and the desired world order? On what basis can we assert the existing one as a pathology? The image of what constitutes a better and more normal world can be very different depending on who is picturing it, even if all of these pictures are equally at odds with our current situation. If you delve into the specifics of each of these alternatives projects, controversies will inevitably arise within the camp of those who support a global alternative. Their unity will be shaken, their will to resist will be paralyzed, and competition between their various projects will undermine the consolidation of anti-globalist forces. We must resist this tendency. Thus, a normal world, a better world, must be talked of only with the utmost caution. Nevertheless, there are some very obvious principles and benchmarks which can hardly be questioned by anyone in their right mind. Let's try to find them.

a. *An economic model is required, an alternative to the system of speculative financial capitalism that exists today.* Alternatives can be seen in "real industrial capitalism," in Islamic economics, in socialism, in Green projects, and in systems that are linked to actual production. We must search for completely new economic mechanisms, including new forms of energy, labor organization, and so on. The economy of a normal world will not be the same as that which exists today.

b. *Recognizing limits to growth and finite natural resources, the distribution problem must be addressed on the basis of a plan that is applicable and common to all mankind,* not on the basis of an egoistic and Darwinian competitive struggle for the use and control of these resources. Resource wars – whether military or economic – must be completely suppressed. Humanity is threatened by this struggle, and in the face of this fact, we have to adopt a different attitude to the issues of democracy and resources. In this game there can be no winners. Everyone will lose. In a normal world, this threat should be answered by all the people of the world together, not separately.

c. *The normal and best state of human existence is not fragmentation and dissipation into atomized individuals, but the preservation of social collective structures which maintain the transmission of culture, knowledge, languages, practices, and beliefs from one generation to the next.* Man is first and foremost a social being — that's why liberal individualism is destructive and criminal. We must save human society at any cost. From this it follows that a social orientation must prevail over the liberal individualism.

d. *In the society which is to take shape, one should be free to preserve his human dignity, his identity, his essence, and his wholeness. We also need to preserve those structures without which an individual personality cannot develop and take root – the family, productive work, public institutions, the right to determine one's own destiny, and so on.* Those trends which are leading to the dissolution of what makes us human as members of societies and cultures, and to its displacement by new, universal human types or posthuman perversions should be stopped. Our humanity in all its existing forms and diversity is something that should be preserved, and even recreated as it once was.

e. *A normal society is one in which peoples, nations and states are preserved as traditional forms of human community — as* created *forms, created by history and tradition.* They can change, but they should not be abolished or forcibly merged into a single global melting pot. The diversity of peoples and nations is a historical treasure of mankind. Abolishing it will be akin to the abolition of history, of freedom, and of cultural wealth. The processes of homogenizing globalization driven by markets must be stopped and reversed.

f. *Normal society is based on the possibility of acquiring knowledge, of giving knowledge, on a form of osmosis with our world and our existence as human* *beings on the basis of tradition, experience, discovery, and the freedom to search for meaning.* The sphere of knowledge should not be a field of virtual pageants, of mass media hypnosis or a space for the manipulation of consciousness on a global scale. The mass media acts as a virtual surrogate that substitutes for reality. This must be replaced by sober self-reflection based on open sources, intuition, creativity, and experience. To achieve this it is necessary to crush the current dictatorship of the mass commercial media and to break up the monopoly of the global elites who currently determine the mass consciousness.

g. *Normal society should have a positive vision of the future.* But at the same time, in order to achieve the intended purpose, it is necessary to abandon the delusion that things in themselves are developing well or, on the contrary, the assumption that catastrophe is inevitable. The point of human history is that it is open. It includes human will and the ability to implement one's own freedom. This makes the future a zone of possibilities: it can be better or worse, depending on how we create it. It all depends on what we choose and what we do. If we don't make a choice or if we lack the will to follow through on it, the future may not come at all, or else that future may not be the one that we prefer.

h. *Normal society must be diverse, plural, and polycentric.* It must contain many open possibilities and many cultures. Dialogue must be free, not forced. Each society must choose for itself the balance between spiritual and material components. Yet as history shows, the sharp domination of materialism invariably leads to disaster. Neglecting the spiritual dimension of our existence is fatal and denies what makes us human. The current abrupt lurch towards exaggerated materialism must be offset by a sharp turn towards the spiritual principle. The domination of wealth and its pursuit must absolutely not supersede other values or be placed on the highest pedestal of a society. Every society in which the role of money is not as great as ours is, by definition, more normal, fair, and acceptable than the one in which we live today. Anyone who thinks otherwise is either sick or is an agent of influence of the global oligarchy. Justice and harmony are more important than personal success and greed. Greed and individualist self-interest are considered a sin or a weakness by nearly every human culture and religion. Justice and concern for the common good is one of the most common values. A just society is more normal than one that is based on selfishness. A normal world order recognizes the balance of power and the right of different societies and cultures to find their own way. That is to say, this is the norm, and this norm, even in most general and approximate form, radically contrasts with what we have around us. This status quo is not normal, it is a pathology. Once the global oligarchy's power is disrupted, all things will return to focus.

3.   In a normal society, we cannot do without power in general. In one or another form it was, is, and will be. It is also present in the global society that exists today. This power belongs to a global oligarchy that veils its exercise of power under the guise of free markets, democracy, complicity, and the façade of a diversity of global decision-making centers. Global oligarchy retains power in every sense, but only indirectly, acting not by coercion, but with subtle means of control. It is less coarse than other forms of power, but is more insidious, deceitful, and sneaky, but no less brutal and totalitarian. Occasionally it takes the form of a paradoxical totalitarian anarchism, giving full freedom to the masses, but only while maintaining complete control over the content, context, and parameters of this freedom. You can do anything, but only in accordance with the established rules. The rules are dictated by the global oligarchy. In a normal society, power should not be held by an anonymous political and financial elite that steadily leads humanity to its end, but to the best in a meritocratic sense — the strongest, smartest, most spiritual and fair, the heroes and sages, but not to a system that rewards the basest of human emotions, greed — the corrupt officials across the globe, and the liars and usurpers. Power always involves the projection of multiple wills to a single instance. The formation of this instance should proceed in accordance with the historical, social, cultural, and sometimes the religious traditions of each particular society. There is no general formula for optimal power. Democracy works in one society and is a fiasco in another. Monarchy may be harmonious, or may become tyranny. Collective management provides both positive and negative results. There are no universal recipes that are suitable for all. But any power, and even the lack of it, is better than that which exists today and which seized control over global humanity.

4.   The standard comes from a particular history of a particular human society, and it should not be replaced by any other. It must be an evolutionary and organic process of historical and cultural development. The norms, the ideals, and the laws that societies and peoples acquire through collective suffering, trials, errors, dialogue, assessment, and experiments are developed over the course of centuries. That's why each particular society has the inalienable right for its own norms and values. No outsider has the right to criticize these norms on the basis of his own, distinct from others. If peoples and nations do not develop in the same way as their neighbors do, it does not means that they simply cannot do so, but that they *in extenso* don't want to, that they reckon historical time and the judgment of successes and failures according to other criteria. This should be avowed once and for all, and any colonial and racist prejudices should be categorically rejected: if some society is dissimilar to ours, it doesn't mean that it is worse, more backward, or primitive; it's just different, and its otherness is its nature. We must avow this. Only such an approach is normal. Globalism, West-centrism and universalism are profound pathologies requiring eradication. Most especially it is pathological or even criminal if universal standards are defined by an illegitimate, self-proclaimed global elite that has usurped global power. There are as many different norms as there are societies. In other words, only one norm is universal: the absence of a uniform standard for all, as well as freedom and the right to choose.

Part Three: The Imperative for Revolution

1.   Against the existing order, which we perceive as an intolerable evil, as a pathology, and as the crisis which will inevitably lead to catastrophe and to the suicide of civilization, it is necessary to propose an *alternative beau ideal* — the standard and the project of that which doesn't currently exist, but of what should be. Thus it is a normative project. But the global oligarchy will not give up its power willingly under any circumstances. It would be naïve to think otherwise. Hence, the task is to dislodge it from its position, to wrest power away from it and to take it by force. This can be done only under one condition: if all the forces that are dissatisfied with the current situation act together. This principle of concerted action is a unique phenomenon in recent history, which has become global. Global oligarchy sets its dominance

on the planetary level. Its global nature is not a secondary quality, but reflects its essence. This global oligarchy attacks all peoples, nations, states, cultures, religions, and societies. There are not any particular types of societies that it attacks, not only some types of regimes, nor any other particular entities singled out for attack. This elite comes frontally and totally, seeking to turn all the areas of the Earth into the zone of its hegemony. The problem is that in these areas there are different societies, different cultures, different peoples, and different religions that haven't yet completely lost their unique natures. Globalization brings cultural death to all of them, and they understand or feel it intuitively. But in the current situation no country on its own has enough power to put up effective resistance against the global oligarchy. Even if you combine the efforts of one or another culture, or one or another regional community, beyond the borders of a single country, their combined forces are still far from equal to the task. Only if all humanity becomes aware of the need for radical opposition to globalism will there be a chance to make our struggle effective and with a successful outcome. Joint action does not require us to be fighting for the same ideals or to be in solidarity with particular standards that will replace the current catastrophe and pathology. These ideals may be different, and even, to some degree, conflict with one another, but we all must realize that if we won't be able to terminate the global oligarchy, all of these projects, whatever they are, will remain unrealized, and we will perish in vain. If we find enough intelligence, will, sobriety, and courage in ourselves to act together against global oligarchy within the framework of a Global Revolutionary Alliance, we will have a chance, an open opportunity not only to fight on equal footing, but also to win. The differences between our societies and their norms will matter only after we overthrow the global oligarchy. Resistance to hegemony is the first and only imperative. Until the hegemony is effectively neutralized or marginalized, the contradictions of the various societal projects will only play into the hands of the global oligarchy, acting on the age-old principle of all empires — "divide and conquer." The global revolution has two aspects: the unity of what is to be destroyed, and the multiplicity of what is to be built in its place.

2.   *The revolution of the twenty-first century cannot be a simple reiteration of the revolutions of the nineteenth or twentieth centuries.* Earlier revolu-

tions sometimes correctly evaluated the flaws of the regimes against which
they were directed, but historical circumstances did not allow them to realize the most versatile and deep roots of evil. The assaults on the truly pathological features of the modern global sociopolitical setup were judged unfair-
ly, alienated and usurped power, and mingled minor and incidental historical
and sociological elements that did not deserve such a harsh rejection. Earlier
revolutions quite often missed the mark rather than hitting the evil, and they
weakened or destroyed things which, on the contrary, often deserved preservation and restoration. This pure evil in its previous phases was hidden
and camouflaged, and sometimes these revolutions themselves contained
elements of its spirit which helped lead to today to the global oligarchic
tyranny which works through both the financial and media sectors, among
others. Moreover, previous revolutions most often proceeded within the
bounds of local conditions, and even when they claimed to be global, they
never had such a scale. Only today are the conditions ripe for a revolution
to become truly global, since the system against which it is directed is already global in practice, not only in theory. Another feature of previous
revolutions was that they put forward clear alternative sociopolitical models, which most often pretended or aspired to universality. If we repeat these
paths today, we will inevitably repel from the revolution many who are looking for an alternative through the prism of their society, history or culture.
Such people want a different future for themselves, but also different from
the other revolutionaries that have been attempted against the global oligarchy. Thence, the revolution of the twenty-first century must be truly planetary and plural in its ultimate goals. All nations of the Earth must revolt against the existing world order jointly, working in tandem, but in the
name of different ideals and reflecting different norms. To have a future, we
must conceive of it as a complex bouquet of opportunities, the realization
of which is being prevented by the current world order and the global oligarchy. If we don't all crush it together in the name of our different purposes and different horizons, we won't get the bouquet, nor any other future.
Let each society fight for its own vision of the future. The revolution of the
twenty-first century will be successful only if all nations will fight against the
common enemy in the name of their different goals, but within its overall
framework.

3. The spectacles that we see today in the so-called "color revolutions" have
    nothing of a genuine revolutionary character. They are organized by the
    global oligarchy and are prepared and supported by its networks. The "color
    revolutions" are almost always aimed against those societies or those politi-
    cal regimes that actively or passively resist the global oligarchy, challenge its
    interests, and try to maintain some independence in matters of policy,
    strategy, regional affairs, and economic measures. Thus, "color revolutions"
    occur selectively, organized via mass media networks deployed by the glo-
    balist elite. These are a twisted parody of revolution, and serve only counter-
    revolutionary purposes.

4. The new revolution should be geared to the radical overthrow of the glob-
    al oligarchy and the destruction of the world's elite, and toward dismantling
    the entire world system associated with it (or, rather, their controlled dis-
    order of things). Destroying the heart of the beast will liberate all peoples
    and societies from this parasitic vampire of global oligarchy. Only this
    can open up the prospect of constructing an alternative future. By its very
    definition, genuine revolution must be global. Global oligarchy is now dis-
    persed throughout the world. It is present not only in the form of a hierar-
    chical structure with a clearly defined center, but in the form of a network
    spread across the world. The center of decision-making is not necessarily
    in the place where the visible centers of the political and strategic manage-
    ment of the West lie – that is, in the US and other centers of the Western
    world. The specific nature of the global transnationalist elite is that its loca-
    tion is mobile and fluid, and its decision-making center is mobile and dis-
    persed. Thus, it is extremely difficult to strike at the core of global oligar-
    chy, focusing only on its territoriality. To defeat this networked evil, it is
    necessary to uproot its presence simultaneously in different parts of the
    Earth. Moreover, it is necessary to infiltrate the network itself, to sow panic,
    cause it to crash, and to infect it with viruses and other destructive process-
    es. A radial destruction of the global oligarchy requires the revolutionary
    forces to master the network's procedures and to study its protocols. Hu-
    manity must fight the enemy on its own territory, because today the entire
    globe is controlled in one way or another by the enemy. The struggle for the
    destruction of the global elite must therefore not only be a common one, but
    also synchronized in different parts of the world, albeit asymmetrically. In

addition, the revolution today necessitates a strategy of guerrilla warfare in the territory occupied by the enemy. Particularly, this means that the battle must be fought in cyberspace as well. Cyber revolution and the practice of radical struggle in virtual reality must be an integral part of the revolution of the twenty-first century.

5.   Of all the ideologies of modernity up to the present time, only one has survived, embodied in *liberalism* or *liberal capitalism*. It is exactly in this where the worldview and *ideological matrix* of global oligarchy is concentrated. This global oligarchy is openly or covertly liberal. Liberalism performs a dual function: on the one hand, it serves as a philosophical cover which strengthens, preserves, and expands the power of the global oligarchy; that is, it acts as a means by which to judge ongoing global politics. On the other hand it enables the recruitment of volunteers and collaborators anywhere in the world who accept the tenets and values of liberalism: political leaders, bureaucrats, industrialists, traders, intellectuals, the scientific community, and youth, all regardless of citizenship or nationality. Liberalism automatically generates the environment in which the staff of globalism is being recruited, via which networks are constructed, information is collected, centers of influence are organized, lobbying is done for the benefit of transnational corporations, and other strategic operations for establishing the global domination of the global oligarchy are conducted. That's why the main focus of the revolution should be on the liberals in all their expressions – as representatives of the ideological, political, economic, philosophical, cultural, strategic, and technological dimensions. Liberals are the shell under which the global oligarchy is hidden. Any strike on liberalism and liberals has a good chance of affecting sensitive parts of the global oligarchy and its vital organs. A total war against liberalism and liberals is the main ideological vector of global revolution. The revolution must be of a rigidly anti-liberal character, because liberalism is a concentrated knot of evil. Any and all other political ideologies can be considered as a legitimate alternative, and there are no restrictions. The only exception is liberalism, which must be destroyed, crushed, overthrown, and made obsolete.

Part Four: The Fall of the West—the United States as a Country of Absolute Evil

1. The origins of the current situation lie deep in the history of the West and the sociopolitical processes that are unfolding in this part of the world. The history of Western Europe led its societies to the point where individualism, rationalism, materialism, and economic reductionism gradually began to dominate, and then on this basis capitalism formed and the bourgeoisie became triumphant. The ideology of liberalism became the ultimate expression of the bourgeois system. Exactly this ideological, philosophical, political, and economic line led to the current situation. At the time of modernity, Europe was the cradle of a materialistic liberal civilization, which it imposed on the other peoples of the Earth through its colonialist and imperialist policies. To this end the most heinous forms of coercion were used: for example, in the sixteenth century Europeans recreated the institution of slavery, which had ceased to exist a thousand years earlier under the influence of Christian ethics. Europeans turned to this disgusting practice at the very moment when the West began to develop the theories of humanism, free thought and democracy. Slavery, therefore, was an innovation of capitalism and the bourgeois order. The bourgeois system was installed in Europe's colonies; in some of them it achieved its most consistent and vivid expression, bringing the bourgeois-democratic path to its logical end. The United States of America, a colonial state based on slavery, individualism, egoism, and the dominance of money and materialism, became the apex of this bourgeois Western civilization of the modern era. Gradually, the former European colonies became independent centers of power and, in the middle of the twentieth century, became the center of all of Western civilization and the pole around which the global capitalist system revolves. After the collapse of the Soviet Union, the power of the US was no longer balanced by that of the socialist bloc and became the unchallenged center of the global bourgeois system. Those in the American elite were the charter members of global oligarchy, and practically defined it. Although today the global oligarchy consists of much more than only the American political class, it also includes the European oligarchy and the partially Westernized bourgeois elites from other parts of the world. The United States became the backbone of the modern global world order around which the rest was structured. American military power is a major strategic factor in global politics, the American economic system is a model for the rest of the world, the American mass media actually amounts to a global network, American cultural clichés are imitated and aped throughout the world, and American technological advances are at the forefront of global technological development. In this way the population of the US itself plays the role of passive hostages being controlled by the global elite, which are using the tools of the American state to implement its global objectives. The United States is a giant golem, controlled by the oligarchy. It embodies the spirit of the global order, which poses an imminent catastrophe in itself and is an expression of evil, injustice, oppression, exploitation, alienation, colonialism, and imperialism.

2.   The United States and its policies around the world is a terrible scourge and a major factor in upholding and strengthening the existing order of things. All the catastrophic trends of our time stem from this foundation.

a.   The American economy is based on the dominance of the financial sector, which completely supplanted the value of industrial production and agriculture. The vast majority of American citizens are employed in the tertiary service sector; they produce nothing concrete. America's financial parasitism applies to the entire planet, because the dollar, which printed without any limitations by its Federal Reserve System, is the primary global reserve currency. The world economy is US-centric and works for the benefit of US interests regardless of whether this economy is effective and efficient or not.

b.   The United States presently consumes the largest percentage of the world's resource reserves per capita, contaminating the atmosphere with toxic waste and throwing billions of tons of debris into the environment. The US uses up resources from the rest of the world and establishes control over its suppliers through its military-strategic, diplomatic, and economic dominance. Hence, the US can set the global prices for a commodity from which the United States itself usually benefits. This model of American world hegemony creates a major imbalance in the world economy, as well as injustice and exploitation, and draws us closer to the inevitable collapse of resources. The distribution of natural resources around the world by the US is guided solely by the interests of the US or the transnational elite, a prerequisite for the impending global catastrophe. American society has gone further than any other Western society along the path of atomization, individualization, and the disruption of social ties. Built by immigrants from all over the world, American society initiated the beginnings of the worship of individual identity. Divorced from a specific collective and from its roots, the West European model was allowed to be reach its culmination in the territory of the Americas in perfect laboratory conditions. American society did not just gradually disintegrate into atomized individuals, but was always composed of them. That's why individualism reached its logical conclusion in the US and why the socialist states lagged far behind the US and the West in this process.

d. It is in the US where the process of individualization has reached its extreme limits and is progressing forward with experiments to develop post-human beings, known as transhumanism. The successes of American scientists in the spheres of cloning, genetic engineering, and hybridization suggest that one day we will witness the appearance of genuine post-human beings.

e. American society was originally based on a mixture of cultures, nations, and ethnic groups according to the principle of the "melting pot." The absence of organic ethnic ties was the result of this process. Spreading its influence throughout the rest of the world, the US also promotes this cosmopolitan principle, proclaiming it a universal norm. Furthermore, the US acts as its driving force, routinely depriving one country after another of their right of national sovereignty and non-interference in domestic affairs whenever it is appropriate to its interests. The US/NATO invasions and occupations of Serbia, Afghanistan, Iraq, and Libya are examples of this in practice. The US plays the major role in promoting cosmopolitism and the de-sovereignization of nations and states.

f. The global mass media, on whose conscience lies the creation of absolutely false virtual images of the world in accordance with the interests of the global oligarchy, are mostly American and represent a continuation of American media and policies. Acting in the interests of the global transnational elite, they base their way of doing things on the US information network. In the American society itself the general population is extremely ignorant and exhibits a lack of culture, combined with their naïvety of trusting in entirely false, deceptive, and fabricated notions that are disseminated by the entertainment industry, the media, and other means. This archetype of ignorance, which is a cartoon representation of the world, society, history, and so on, is spread by the US in tandem with its export of American technology and skills to those countries which fall into the grip of its hegemony. The American system of knowledge, which is focused exclusively on pragmatic and material interests, is based primarily on the exploitation of intellectuals and is almost entirely composed of immigrants from other countries. It represents the culmination of the distortion of the sphere of knowledge for the sake of propaganda, as well as pecuniary and utilitarian benefits.

g. Americans have a very specific conception of progress. They believe in the unlimited growth potential of their economic system and are confident about the future, which from their point of view should be "American." Most of them sincerely believe an expansion of the "American way of life" to all of humanity to be a real boon and goal, and are perplexed when faced with rejection and an entirely different, negative reaction (especially when the spread of this lifestyle is accompanied by a military invasion and mass extermination of the local population, the violent uprooting of traditional and religious customs, and other delights of direct occupation). What Americans call "progress" — the "democratization," "development" and "civilizing" of the rest of the world is in fact a degradation, colonization, degeneration, degeneracy and paradoxically a peculiar form of liberal dictatorship. It is no exaggeration to say that the United States is a stronghold of militant liberalism, a visible embodiment and progenitor of all the evil that plagues humanity today, and a powerful mechanism that steadily leads humanity towards the final catastrophe. This is the empire of absolute evil. The hostages and victims of the disastrous course of this empire are not only all other nations, but also ordinary Americans, who are no different from the rest of the conquered, fleeced, deprived and persecuted peoples of the Earth. They, too, are part of the slaughter of nations.

3. It is significant that the national symbols of America are quite sinister in form. The Statue of Liberty resembles the Greek goddess of hell, Hecate, and her torch, which is lit up at night, alludes to the fact that this is a country of night. The dollar sign resembles the Pillars of Hercules, beyond which, according to the ancient Greeks, was the region of Atlantis — that of titans and

demons which sank because of its pride, materialism and corruption. However, instead of the inscription *Nec plus ultra*, or "nothing beyond," which was made on an aegis upon the columns, the Americans have put the inscription *Plus ultra*, or "further beyond." They have thus broken a symbolic ban in the process of morally justifying the construction of their hellish civilization. The Masonic pyramid appears on the Great Seal of the United States, but has no top, symbolizing a society without a vertical hierarchy that is cut off from its heavenly source. No less ominous are its other symbols. These are details, and they can be looked at in different ways, but knowing what a huge role they play in human culture, at the same time we must not neglect such significant symbols.

4.   The US leads other societies to ruin and perishes itself. At the same time, the scale of the catastrophic processes is such that it would be naïve to expect that someone in this situation would be able to wriggle out from under the destructive power of the falling idol alone. The question is not to simply "push the falling one" but to nudge it to such a place that we are out of danger so that it does not crush us. The American Tower of Babel is destined to collapse, but it is very likely that all other countries will be buried under its rubble. The US became a global phenomenon long ago. It is not an isolated country. Therefore, the struggle with the United States cannot be of the same character as those historical wars that were waged by one state against others or against coalitions of states. America is a planetary phenomenon, the global hyperpower, and an effective fight against it is possible only if it will take place simultaneously throughout the world. This includes fighting within the territory of the US itself, where, as elsewhere, nonconformist revolutionary forces that categorically disagree with the direction of the United States, the capitalist world, and the global West are present. These revolutionary forces within the US may be the most diverse groups - both Rightists and Leftists, and people of different religious, ethnic, and religious orientations. They must be regarded as a valuable segment of the planetary revolutionary front. To some extent we are all today in the American empire, either directly or indirectly, and it is still unknown whether it is easier and safer to struggle against it on the periphery or in those countries that have not yet been formally placed under direct American control. The suite of global oligarchy, which is almost always at the same time agents

of American influence and either hidden or outright liberals, is alert to dem-
onstrations of non-conformism throughout the world. With the prolifera-
tion of extremely effective tracking methods, enormous data storage capacity, and ultra-fast information processing and transmission, the continuous
shadowing of any suspicious element anywhere in the world, and at any time,
is already a matter of ease, and tomorrow it will be a routine occurrence. It
is important to understand that we live in a global America, and in this respect, those who oppose the United States and American hegemony as well
as the global oligarchy from the outside don't differ much from those who are
aligned against the same enemies from within their ostensible borders. We
are all in the same situation.

5.   The United States and the elements behind disembodied transnational
finance are the poles of the catastrophic processes that are inevitably leading humanity and the global system to commit suicide, and as such are the
basis for all forces opposed to the status quo to join into a single, global anti-
American front. A movement comprising all of humanity should be created, the network and structure of which would unite all those who want
to see the fall of the US and who are ready to take some part in the struggle to make it happen. This is not about America as a country, but about
Americanism as a principle. It is not about the American state, but about
the structural core of a global network of subjugation, submission, deceit,
and parasitism. It is not about the American masses, but about the global oligarchic elites that control them. Nowadays, the US is responsible for everything. Thus it must be destroyed as a historical, political, social, military,
and strategic phenomenon. But how this can be achieved despite the fact
that in the fields of the military, finance, technology, economics, and aggressive cultural expansion, the US is now the undisputed leader of the world
in all its aspects? Those countries that are critical of the United States are
afraid to even discuss a direct confrontation with the planetary monster in
a purely theoretical way while it still retains its enormous destructive power.
A direct frontal attack will clearly not resolve this problem. The war with
the United States should be conducted at a different level, according to new
rules and by using new strategies, technologies, and methods.

Part Five: Practice for War

1.   The global oligarchy exploits convenient conflicts and divides and incites its enemies against each other. It provokes and wages aggressive wars and will continue to act this way in the future. The question is not, "to fight or not to fight." We will be forced to fight in any case. Today the more important question is how to fight and with whom? War is an indefeasible part of human history. All attempts to evade it in practice have led only to new wars, each time more violent than the previous ones. Thus, realism compels us to treat war evenly and impartially. Humanity has always waged wars, wages them now, and will wage them until its end. Many of the religious prophecies about the end of the world describe it in terms of a "final battle." Thus, war must be understood as a socio-cultural environ of human existence. It is inevitable and this should be taken for granted. Wars will rend humanity, but we must learn to correctly analyze the forces involved in each war. This analysis qualitatively changes under our current circumstances. Earlier wars were fought between ethnic groups, or between religions, or between empires, or between national states. In the twentieth century, wars were fought between ideological blocs. Today a new era of warfare has come, where the protagonist is always the global oligarchy, carrying out its plans, either with the direct use of American forces and NATO troops, or by organizing local conflicts in such a way that its scenario is consistent with the interests of this elite, albeit indirectly. In some cases, conflicts, wars, and unrest are provoked with the participation of many groups, none of which represent the interests of the global oligarchy directly; then we are dealing with a situation of controlled chaos, the design and aim of which American strategists first developed in the 1980s. In other cases, the global oligarchy stands simultaneously on both sides of the two warring parties, manipulating them to its advantage. A correct analysis of modern war is thus reduced to defining the algorithm of this behavior and singling out the tactical and strategic goals of the global oligarchy and the American state in each particular case. This sort of analytics requires a new methodology derived from a revolutionary and global consciousness. Whether we are participating in a war or watching a war from the outside, we should always try to understand its hidden structure and its true nature and motivations; that is to say, each instance of war encompasses the qualities of practically all of today's wars, with the help of which the global oligarchy maintains and strengthens its dominance, trying to delay its end.

2. Under the conditions of such warfare, an anti-American front must first correctly analyze the opposing forces and the global oligarchy's interests hidden behind them, and secondly, must master the skill of reorienting its military actions against the real culprit in any modern conflict — against the global oligarchy itself, the liberal environment, America's network of agents of influence, and other accomplices. Today there are no longer aggressors and victims, national interests or competition, as explained the wars of the past. The wars of the twenty-first century have a character of episodes in a single, global civil war, insurgency and symmetrical retributive operations. An anti-American front by its very existence should serve as a mechanism for the reorientation of any military conflict that breaks out so that it realizes its true purpose and its real culprits — the US, globalism, and their structures.

3. The new reality of warfare requires us to improve our skills in the classic methods of fighting, as well as mastering new avenues and vehicles of war, including networks, and cyber and virtual zones. Mastering these areas is the most important area for the anti-American front, because virtual networks allow us to effectively use asymmetric forms of warfare. If the resources of the global hierarchy, and their American and NATO tools, in terms of hard military power in the sense of traditional, conventional weapons renders them incomparably and many times far superior to the combined strength of their potential adversaries, then in this area of conflict there is hardly a chance to win. But in the area of network warfare and cyber strategies, other factors are decisive. Not least is the role played by creativity, unconventional ways of thinking, and ingenuity. In cyberspace, at a certain stage, the forces of global oligarchy and the revolutionary counter-elite can be on an equal footing, at least temporarily: within the framework of a new area for conflict, especially in its early stages, the creativity of someone working alone can be comparable to what can be achieved with the enormous budgets of transnational corporations. With a personal Website or a stylish blog, a gifted individual might attract public attention and have an impact comparable to a government's official sources of information, or even of a large-scale project well-funded by the globalist's media empire. Having mastered network strategies,

it becomes possible to wage an excellent and dynamic cyber war against the global oligarchy - including viral campaigns, revolutionary trolling, flaming, flooding, spamming and usage of bots, and socket-puppet strategies. In this regard, an anti-American front of the global counter-elite needs both military trainers and veterans of traditional conflicts, hackers, programmers, and system administrators for the global network of resistance. Reality itself is now the battlefield of the war — both offline and virtual. We must be prepared to lead an all-out global war, extending the zone of our combat operations to all levels – from everyday aspects of behavior, lifestyle, fashion, work, and leisure to ideology, information flows, technology, networking, and virtual worlds. We must seek to inflict the maximum damage possible on the global oligarchy and the interests of the US and NATO on all available levels — personal, military, economic, cultural, informational, network, cyberspace, and so on. The enemy must be attacked both frontally and stealthily. At any point where resistance to globalism sparks, the anti-American front should give support to the rebels in the form of information dissemination and military assistance, and by conducting all manner of actions aimed at inflicting maximal damage on the global oligarchy: moral, physical, informational, ideological, material, economic, in terms of its image, and so on.

4.   The world revolutionary counter-elite must act by any and all means, either military or peaceful ones, depending on the circumstances. It should be clear that we are dealing with a system of illegitimate liberal terror; a political system created by the cannibalistic junta of international maniacs who have unlawfully seized the control levers of the world, leading humanity to suicide. If we accept their rules, we are guaranteed slavery, humiliation, degradation, dissolution, and an inglorious end. The current situation is not just temporary, burdened by unpleasant chance occurrences and vexatious costs; it is a fatal diagnosis: a continuation of present trends is not compatible with long-term survival. In such a situation, there will no longer be law, limits, moral attitudes, or codes of conduct. We shall speak on this topic only after the destruction of the obscene global clique of oligarchs and their international mercenaries has been completed. Thus, in the fight against the system, any means to an end is acceptable and justifiable. We must recognize that the power of the global oligarchy cannot be considered legal or legiti-

mate, and all those who cooperate with or facilitate it are illegitimate collaborators. The only legitimate law is the global revolutionary struggle for a radical change in the course of human history. Only this war is legitimate, just and moral. Only its rules and purposes are justified and worthy of respect. Anyone who is not involved in this war on the side of the Revolution is already helping the global oligarchy to maintain and strengthen their power. The law of modern global society is lawlessness, and all norms have been reversed. The only rightful course today is revolt, resistance, and struggle against the status quo, and trying to put an end to its despotism. While power is in the hands of the global oligarchy, we don't have to comply with any laws except the laws of war and revolution. The global oligarchy itself creates its own law, provoking conflicts and then trying to manipulate them. Under such circumstances, we are dealing with criminals and maniacs. Stopping them is the duty of every normal person who is mindful of the dignity of his species. War is our homeland, our element, and our natural, native environment in which we must learn to exist effectively and victoriously.

Part Six: The Structure of the Global Revolutionary Alliance

1. The subject of the new world revolution must be the worldwide counter-elite. This counter-elite is intended to form the core of the Global Revolutionary Alliance (GRA) as a crystallization of efforts to promote subversive and disruptive revolutionary activities around the world aimed at the demolition of the current global system and the overthrow of the power of the global oligarchy and its entourage. This Global Revolutionary Alliance should be a new type of organization, proper to the conditions of the twenty-first century. It should not be a party, a movement, an order, a lodge, a sect, a religious community, or an ethnic group or caste, as were collective bodies of earlier eras, since they cannot serve as a model for its structure. The Global Revolutionary Alliance should be a new type of organization in the structure of a network, without a single center of authority or a fixed set of permanent members, nor should it have a steering group, a permanent establishment, or a well-defined algorithm of action. The Global Revolutionary Alliance should be spontaneous and organically inscribed in the logic of global processes, never something that is planned in

advance and not tied to a particular time and place. Only such a mobile presence will provide an alliance effectiveness and immunity against the planetary system of oppression and its enforcers. The Alliance's activities should be based on understanding a set of common principles, the objectives of the struggle, the identity of the enemy, and recognizing the status quo as catastrophic, intolerable and requiring total destruction. They must also be based on an understanding of the causes of this situation, the stages of its development and those essential processes that make it possible and very real. Everyone who understands these things, and everyone who doesn't accept the current situation and who is ready to act in accordance with this understanding, is a member of the Global Revolutionary Alliance. That's why it must be polycentric. It shouldn't have a single territorial, national, religious, or any other center. The Alliance should operate everywhere, regardless of frontiers, races, and religions, on the basis of an inner conviction and by spontaneously opening windows of opportunity. The absence of a general strategy shall be the axis of its revolutionary strategy, and the absence of a fixed, hierarchical command center shall be the primary model for its operation. The Global Revolutionary Alliance should be everywhere and nowhere, and should carry out its rebel actions continuously, but never at a fixed time. The Global Revolutionary Alliance should make an appearance only when and where the global oligarchy least expects it. In this, the Global Revolutionary Alliance should be similar to the avant-garde performances, to Zen Buddhist practice, or to an exciting game; a game on which rests nothing less than the fate of humanity. The rules of this game can easily be changed as it develops. The players can change their faces, identity, personal history, and other personal characteristics, including their residences and identification documents. The Global Revolutionary Alliance should provoke a system failure, a short circuit in the functioning of the global hierarchy and its support system. This cannot be carried out in a well-planned, carefully prepared manner; the global oligarchy will immediately discover it and take preventive measures. That's why we should act with a focus on complete unpredictability, combining heroic actions by individuals with collective actions in all aspects of reality.

2. The Global Revolutionary Alliance should be deliberately asymmetric – potentially, states, social forces, political parties, movements, groups, and

even individuals could take part in it. All that opposes the power of the global oligarchy, strongly or moderately, directly or tangentially, must be regarded as a territory of Global Revolutionary Alliance. This area can be conditional or concrete, national or cybernetic, organic or a network.

a. If any country in the world, large or small, acts against the global domination of the US, NATO, the global West and the world liberal financial system, then this state should be considered a part of the Global Revolutionary Alliance and assisted in every way, regardless of whether we share values of this state, whether its rulers are attractive or repulsive, or whether its present political system is just or corrupt. Nothing should keep us from supporting such a state. Given the present balance of powers throughout the world, any criticism, blackening or demonization of such a state can only be black propaganda stemming from the global elites in an attempt to discredit their opponents. The Global Revolutionary Alliance categorically prohibits its supporters and participants from making any criticism of anti-American regimes and even of those countries whose policies, at least in some ways, significantly differ from the strategy of the global elite. Those who will succumb to the ploy of the globalist system of total disinformation, and who believe the insinuations made against such anti-American regimes, deserves to be condemned. In such instances, we cannot rule out the possibility that such criticism is coming from provocateurs who are seeking to split the ranks of the counter-elite. The observance or violation of this rule can be a way to determine the adequacy of those who claim to participate in the Global Revolutionary Alliance.

b. The same principle applies in the case of evaluating movements, parties, and religious, national, or political organizations. It does not matter what they advocate. Whether their goals are good or bad, whether we like or dislike their leaders, or whether their values, attitudes, and motives are clear or not is unimportant. Only one thing matters: whether they fight against the US and the global oligarchy and whether they seek to destroy the existing system, or if, on the contrary, they maintain it, serve it and assist its functioning. The former are automatically considered to be elements of Global Revolutionary Alliance; the latter fall into the camp of the world's evil and are satellites of the global oligarchy, and in that case they should not expect mercy. Special criteria for our orientation towards chaos should be established here: those movements, political parties, religious groups, and other associations which put their competition and conflicts with other movements of a similar inclination above their imperative of opposition to the global oligarchy are indirect accomplices of the oligarchy themselves and are its unconscious instruments. The global oligarchy maliciously incites one group against another to distract both from what should be their primary struggle. That's why only those groups (large ones, as carriers of particular world religions, and small ones, as independent associations of citizens on a common platform) should be allowed to join the ranks of the Global Revolutionary Alliance that are clearly aware of the fact that in any local and regional confrontations, the main enemy is usually hidden. It is the global oligarchy. To defeat it, if necessary, they must unite even with their worst enemies (on the local level), if they are also oriented against this oligarchy. Those who challenge this principle play into the hands of the global oligarchy and can be blamed as accomplices. In this sphere the mass media also cannot be trusted when they discredit certain political, national, ideological or religious organizations that contend with global oligarchy: for certain all the information about them will be false, and to trust any of it should be considered a mistake, if not a crime. Those who are denigrated by the global media are almost certainly the most deserving political, religious, ideological, and social groups and movements for the support of the Global Revolutionary Alliance.

c. The same should be applied to those individuals who reject or criticize the global oligarchy. These are already members of Global Revolutionary Alliance on their own, whether they realize it or not, declare it, or conceal, avow, or deny it. It is not necessary to demand a clear position from such people: for various reasons, in certain situations it would be disadvantageous for them (and thus for all of us). It is necessary only to evaluate the damage that they cause in practice to the global oligarchy and proceed from that. The specific program for which they struggle is absolutely irrelevant. It may be near to ours, or it may be completely different. It is necessary to evaluate these people by the extent and effectiveness of their resistance, their subversion, and their destructiveness to the current status quo. If this level is high, they deserve full and unquestioning support. Again, in this case it would be a mistake, and even a crime, to take into account the derogatory slander that is produced against them by the global media and its national satellites. If the global oligarchy puts a particular person on its blacklists, the Global Revolutionary Alliance simply must support him. Most often everything alleged against this person would be a deliberate falsehood from beginning to end. But this does not matter – even if all the globalists' innuendos were pure truth, it wouldn't change anything. We live under martial law and a hero is that person who is able to inflict maximum damage upon the enemy, but not necessarily someone who has exemplary morals or other qualities that are needed to earn him a good reputation in times of peace. A revolutionary has his own morality: it is the effectiveness and success of his struggle against global despotism.

3.　　Whatever the motives which cause certain powers to reject the status quo and challenge the oligarchy, globalization, liberalism, and the US, they should be brought into the Alliance in any case. The rest will be decided after our victory over the enemy and the collapse of the new Babylon. This is the most important principle that should be taken as the basis of the Global Revolutionary Alliance. The global oligarchy protects its power by relying on the fact that the various projects of those revolutionary forces that oppose it all differ from one another, from one society to another, from one confession — or even between strands of a confession — to another, from one party to another, and finally, from one individual to another. These contradictions in goals and values divide the camp of those who oppose the status quo and thereby create the conditions for continuing domination by the global elite. This principle is the strategic backbone of its despotic power. It has repeatedly been the case that even weak attempts to unite different parties, movements, ethnic groups, states, or individuals on a general anti-globalist and anti-oligarchic platform has caused a hysterical reaction in the global oligarchy and their allies, leading to repressions and preventive measures to eradicate and prevent such efforts. By even discussing the topic of the creation of a Global Revolutionary Alliance, ignoring differences in objectives on the basis of our unity against a common enemy, we hit the most vulnerable spot of the system, break open its code, and undermine the basis of its imperial strategy. The history of the twentieth century shows that any association that is based on common goals, even at its most massive (as was in the case with the global system of

Communism which operated in practically all the countries of the world), has its own restrictive bar and cannot go beyond a certain limit. The collapse of world socialism was related to this: having united everyone possible around anti-capitalist initiatives with clearly defined, positive goals possessing dogmatic foundations which did not allow for other interpretations, the Communists exhausted all the revolutionary resources of Marxism failed to reach the critical mass that was necessary for a decisive victory over capitalism. Fiery strains of conservative, religious, and nationalist movements were left entirely outside the Marxist movement that were equally intransigent in regard to global capitalism but which did not share their specific vision of a Communist utopia. Taking advantage of this split, the West was able to defeat the Soviet bloc. This fate must be taken very seriously into account by revolutionaries of the twenty-first century. If we continue insisting today on absolute agreement on a single purpose that we propose as an alternative to a global capitalist oligarchy and world domination by the US, we will be doomed to inevitable failure and ourselves put a weapon in the hands of the enemy to use against us.

4. The Global Revolutionary Alliance should be fed first of all by a spirit of freedom and independence, and only secondarily should seek material resources for the realization of particular operations and projects. Never start with material concerns or questions of resources. It should start from the will. This is the sense of human dignity. This is the most important rule for the development of the Global Revolutionary Alliance. Spirit should be at its center. There are situations where one cannot cope with external circumstances, with forces of nature, or with the power of fate. Sometimes one is confronted with obstacles that are impossible to overcome. But the essence of humanity lies in the fact that, even when conceding to brute force or the pressure of circumstances, one can morally admit or not what is happening, but can still say either "yes" or "no" to these circumstances. And if he says "no," he thereby sentences circumstance with his decisive verdict, thus preparing the platform for further resolve. In disagreeing with the objective world, the human spirit already transforms it, and even if the consequences of his verdict do not come immediately and do not come for him, it is never without value and meaning. It is exactly this spirit that maintains history, society and human life. Any material wealth and any potential that lacks

the support of this spirit, as well as its accompanying will and moral approval, will be useless and powerless. We know examples where whole civilizations have denied a link between materialism and true values, and which on the contrary place true values in the spiritual realm – in the worlds of contemplation, the deity, faith, and asceticism. Conversely, with the ability to make moral choices, will is able to transform a complete lack of resources and means into its opposite; to construct a vast empire with minimal starting capital, covering a vast area of the material world. The human spirit can do anything. That's why the Global Revolutionary Alliance should be ready to begin its struggle against the global oligarchy on any basis — from a single individual or a small group of people to movements, parties, and such, and even up to the level of entire religious communities, societies, nations, or civilizations. You can charge into a battle with nothing at all on the basis of an understanding of the current situation and a spirit of radical discontent and dissatisfaction with what is happening around you. You can rely on existing structures on any scale that offer support. Resources for the implementation of global revolutionary activities and for a total planetary war should be drawn from everywhere, without concern for their sources or their fates. Here everything can be useful, big and small — traditional weapons and new technologies, and the infrastructures of entire states or international organizations, as well as the creativity of individuals who heroically join the struggle against the global oligarchic beast.

5.   Only the spirit determines human history. In the spirit, in its sickness, in its weakness, in its decline, and in its stupefaction, we should look for the root of our current pathology. It can be cured only by the spirit.

Part Seven: Visions of the Future: The Dialectics of Multiple Norms

1.   The future will be possible *if we manage to destroy the existing world* and to make our norms a reality. Each segment of the anti-American front and each element of the Global Revolutionary Alliance has its own vision of the future and its own norms. It must be assumed that these images and these norms are different, disparate and even mutually exclusive. This situation will only cause problems if each of these norms and visions of the future are viewed by their adherents as something universal and obligatory, becoming

something that excludes that which is common to all mankind. If this happens, a split within the Global Revolutionary will become inevitable, sooner or later. This would doom its activities to failure. The Muslim, atheist, Christian, socialist, anarchist, conservative, libertarian, fundamentalist, sectarian, progressive, ecologist, or traditionalist will never get along with each other if they try to impose their vision of the future onto their neighbors, and beyond them to all of humanity. The global oligarchy will immediately take advantage of it, driving a wedge between each group within the Alliance, splitting their solidarity and leaving each to its destruction. The primitive simplicity of such a strategy has invariably and consistently brought a positive result to those who have used it over the millennia. The Global Revolutionary Alliance has no right to succumb to such a pre-programmed and anticipated tactic. The ability to extract knowledge from history and build a strategy based on rational thought is an essential feature of an intelligent person. Thus, for success in its war, the Global Revolutionary Alliance must avoid this impending trap. With diverse and disparate visions of the future, we must learn to presume to implement them only in their local, rather than a universal, context. Islam for Muslims, Christianity for Christians, socialism for socialists, ecology for environmentalists, fundamentalism for fundamentalists, nation for nationalists, anarchy for anarchists, and so on – this should be our way of designing the future. This means that we must recognize the multiplicity and plurality of the future, and its many variations, as well as the possible coexistence of different designs for the future on different contiguous or non-contiguous territories. The Global Alliance is against the notion of one, common revolutionary future for all. It advocates for a bouquet of the future, for humanity to be replenished by a variety of shades and colors, paths, and variations, horizons and targets, places both for a step forward or a return to one's roots. But for some of these alternatives visions of the future to come into existence, the help of other forces that are sure to envision their future in a different way, is needed. This is the primary innovation of the revolutionary strategy of the twenty-first century. Nobody gets their future if no one else does, or if they reject the other's right to have their own future, distinct from all others with its own norms and horizons. The future will become real and free only if all nations and cultures, all civilizations and political movements, all states and individuals accept this fundamental right to difference, and in so doing find unity in diversity and manage to overthrow American hegemony, the global oligarchy, and the neoliberal financial system. This can be done only by combining the efforts of all the discontented. No one should be excluded from the Global Revolutionary Alliance. All who are against the status quo and who see the root of evil in liberalism, globalism, and Americanism, should be treated as plenipotentiary participants of our common front.

2.   The future must be based on the principle of solidarity and on societies as organic, holistic units. Each culture will come to enshrine its values within a particular spiritual and religious form. This form will be different in each, but they all have something in common: there can be no such thing as genuine cultures, religions, and states, which consider materialism, money, physical comfort, mechanical efficiency and vegetative pleasure to be their highest values. Matter alone can never reproduce its own form — it is formless. But such an absolutely materialistic civilization is being built on a global scale by the global oligarchy, which is exploiting the basest, most tangible incentives and the most primitive impulses of the human being. At the very bottom of the soul sleep shameful, semi-animalistic, semi-demoniac energies which are drawn toward the material world in order to merge with organic, physical beings. These sluggish energies, which are resistant to fire, light, concentration, and elevation, are the very backbone of the machinations being exploited by the global system. It cultivates these things, flattering those who gallivant. This bottom of the soul, or the voice of materialism, ruins any cultural form, any ideal, and any norm, regardless of whatever it is. This means that the course of history stops and the eternal recurrence of the cycle of consumption begins, as does the race for material pleasures and the consumption of seductive and mindless images. This is the way societies lose their future. Every culture opposes these basest appetites and energies of spiritual entropy and decay, but does so in its own way and sets a waymark for its norms, ideas, and spirit. Despite the fact that the lineaments and configurations of these forms and ideals are different, they all have one thing in common – in fact this commonality exists anywhere we are talking about form, not substance; about the idea, and not about physicality; and about norms and exerting effort, but not about dissipation, entertainment, and debauchery. Therefore, the vision of the future for which all the elements of the

Global Revolutionary Alliance fight against the global oligarchy, in all their diversity, is a common one. In all cases, it is the form rather than deformity; an idea, but not matter; something that elevates the human spirit, rather than something that causes it to sink into the abyss of empty, inertial entropic physicality. At the heart of any norm stand a common good, truth, and beauty. Each nation has its own ideals which are often very different. They share the view that there *are* ideals rather than something else. The global oligarchy destroys all these ideals, denying their very existence. In doing so it deprives all societies of the future.

3. Our will shall be discovered in the war and it will harden in the fire of revolution. It won't occur simply by itself. That's why the revolution against the American vision of a globalized world is not just a detail or an accident, but is the sense of the work of history, whose movement is being blocked by certain forces. These forces will not go away by themselves, will not step aside, and will not give way for the energies of existence. We are in a civilizational and historical dead end, and the structure of this dead end is such that it has as both an objective and subjective dimension; that is, the deadlock is deliberately and selfishly maintained by certain historical, and at the same time anti-historical, phenomena: the global oligarchy. To open the gates to the future, it is necessary to blow up the dam that stands in its way. No war — no victory. No victory — no future. Unlike in nature, in which the Sun rises every morning, the onset of the dawn of human history depends directly on the effectiveness and success of the struggle against the dark forces: the world oligarchy, the US, and global capitalism. Only by uprooting the existing global elite can the course of history be allowed to move forward from where it is stuck today. The future can only be created in the war and born out of the fire of the Global Revolution. The War and Revolution are an awakening. The daytime is the time of the awakened ones. Meanwhile, the global oligarchy does all it can to ensure that humanity continues sleeping and seeks to ensure that it never awakes. For this purpose an artificial, virtual world is being created, where night lasts forever and the daytime is visible only in an exquisite electronic simulation. This world should be destroyed and replaced.

4. The design of the future must be contemplated and created *openly*. Peoples and societies must select it, rather than it being something im-

posed. Thus, the Global Revolutionary Alliance should appeal to all and to everyone, revealing everything about its goals and objectives, its horizons, and its plans. The Global Revolutionary Alliance should not impose anything on anyone, and does not seek to coerce. The Global Revolutionary Alliance promises nothing, doesn't tempt, and doesn't lead toward a goal that is clear to its adherents but that remains a mystery to everyone else. Such tactics will not give us the desired result. The Global Revolutionary Alliance insists on a universal awakening, on total mobilization, and on the piercing and general awareness of the catastrophe that has overtaken us and which is gaining momentum. On this tragic foundation we must build a new, transparent world that is open to all people. We must tell people the truth: the state of humanity is awful; the self-diagnosis is most disappointing. Yes, this is a disease, a severe illness, deep and relentless. But...still curable. It is curable if it is recognized for what it is: as a disease, considered as such and if there is the will to change the situation and to do what is necessary for recovery. To get healthy, it is necessary to recover. To recover, we must realize that we are seriously ill. The first step toward recovery will be to identify what the disease is doing to us and what are its main carriers. We can study the case records of Western culture in modern times and in the historical prelude of modernity. The carrier of the disease, which is as parasitic on modernity's development as tumor cells are in healthy tissues, is the global oligarchy, the State-Monster of the US, the ideology of liberalism. It is vicious at its foundations, the worldwide network of its agents of influence that serve the interests of the empire of evil in all societies, including those which were able to maintain at least partial immunity to these malignant, corrosive viruses. Doctors know that without the patient's will to recover, it is not possible to do it, and no tricks or other, external methods will help. Therefore, the principal allies of the Global Revolutionary Alliance to come are people in themselves: societies, cultures, and the whole of humanity, which is simply obliged to wake up and shake off the blood-sucking American oligarchic, liberal scum. It is time to hit reset and start living a full life, according to one's own will and relying on one's own mind. Then the mission of the Global Revolutionary Alliance will be carried out and there will no longer be a need for it. In its place the future will come, a future which mankind will have chosen for itself, and which it will freely make with its own hands. It will create itself, by itself and for itself only.

On "White Nationalism" and Other Potential Allies in the Global Revolution

There are different tendencies in the new generation of revolutionary, non-conformist movements in Europe (on the Right as well as the Left), and some of them have been successful in attaining high political positions in their respective countries. The crisis of the West will grow broader and deeper every day, so we should expect an increase in the power and influence of our own Eurasianist resistance movement against the present global order, which is a dictatorship by the worst elements of the Western societies.

Those from either the Right or the Left who refuse American hegemony, ultra-liberalism, strategic Atlanticism, the domination of oligarchic and cosmopolitan financial elites, individualistic anthropology, and the ideology of human rights, as well as typically Western racism in all spheres — economic, cultural, ethical, moral, biological and so on — and who are ready to cooperate with Eurasian forces in defending multipolarity, socio-economic pluralism, and a dialogue among civilizations, we consider to be allies and friends.

Those on the Right who support the United States, White racism against the Third World, who are anti-socialist and pro-liberal, and who are willing to collaborate with the Atlanticists; as well as those on the Left who attack Tradition, the organic values of religion and the family, and who promote other types of social deviations — both of these are in the camp of foe.

In order to win against our common enemy, we need to overcome the ancient hatreds between our peoples, as well as those between the obsolete political ideologies that still divide us. We can resolve such problems amongst ourselves after our victory.

At the present time, we are ALL being challenged, and ALL of us are being dominated by the forces of the prevailing global order.

Before we concern ourselves with these other issues, we first need to liberate ourselves.

I am very happy that Gábor Vona, whom I have met, and who is the leader of the Jobbik party in Hungary, understands this perfectly. We need to be united in creating a common Eurasian Front.

In Greece, our partners could eventually be Leftists from SYRIZA, which refuses Atlanticism, liberalism and the domination of the forces of global finance. As far as I know, SYRIZA is anti-capitalist and it is critical of the global oligarchy that has victimized Greece and Cyprus. The case of SYRIZA is interesting because of its far-Left attitude toward the liberal global system. It is a good sign that such non-conformist forces have appeared on the scene. Dimitris Konstakopulous writes excellent articles and his strategic analysis I find very correct and profound in many cases.

There are also many other groups and movements with whom we can work. The case of the Golden Dawn (Chrysi Avgi) is interesting because it is part of the growing (and very exciting indeed) reappearance of radical Right parties in the European political landscape. We need to collaborate with all forces, Right or Left, who share our principles.

The most important factor should not be whether these groups are pro-Russian or not. What they oppose is of much greater importance here. The enemy of my enemy is my friend. It is simple and easy to understand. If we adopt such an attitude in order to appeal to all possible allies (who either approve of us or who do not), more and more people will follow suit — if only due to pragmatism. In doing so, we will create a real, functioning network — a kind of Global Revolutionary Alliance. It is important that we pursue a strategy of uniting the Left and the Right everywhere, including in the United States. We need to save America from its own dictatorship, which is as bad for the American people as it is for all other peoples.

The issue of limited or unlimited government is, as far as I can see, of lesser importance in comparison with geopolitics — it all depends on the historical tradition of the nation in question. Gun ownership is a good thing when the guns are in our hands. Therefore, these two points when taken as a political platform I consider to be absolutely neutral in themselves. Such an American Right can be good or bad, depending on other factors beyond these two points. We need to have a dialogue with those who look deeper into the nature of things, into history and who try to understand the present world order.

I consider the "White nationalists" allies when they refuse modernity, the global oligarchy and liberal-capitalism, in other words everything that is killing all ethnic cultures and traditions. The modern political order is essentially globalist and based entirely on the primacy of individual identity in opposition to community. It is the worst order that has ever existed and it should be totally destroyed. When "White nationalists" reaffirm Tradition and the ancient culture of the European peoples, they are right. But when they attack immigrants, Muslims or the nationalists of other countries based on historical conflicts; or when they defend the United States, Atlanticism, liberalism or modernity; or when they consider the White race (the one which produced modernity in its essential features) as being the highest and other races as inferior, I disagree with them completely.

More than this, I can't defend Whites when they are in opposition to non-Whites because, being White and Indo-European myself, I recognize the differences of other ethnic groups as being a natural thing, and do not believe in any hierarchy among peoples, because there is not and cannot be any common, universal measure by which to measure and compare the various forms of ethnic societies or their value systems. I am proud to be Russian exactly as Americans, Africans, Arabs, or Chinese are proud to be what they are. It is our right and our dignity to affirm our identity, not in opposition to each other but such as it is: without resentment against others or feelings of self-pity.

I can't defend the concept of the nation, because the idea of the "nation" is a bourgeois concept concocted as a part of modernity in order to destroy traditional societies (empires) and religions, and to replace them with artificial pseudo-communities based on the notion of individualism. All of that is wrong. The concept of the nation is now being destroyed by the same forces that created it, back during the first stage of modernity. The nations have already fulfilled their mission of destroying any organic and spiritual identity, and now the capitalists are liquidating the instrument they used to achieve this in favor of direct globalization. We need to attack capitalism as the absolute enemy which was responsible for the creation of the nation as a simulacrum of traditional society, and which was also responsible for its destruction. The reasons behind the present catastrophe lie deep in the ideological and philosophical basis of the modern world. In the beginning, modernity was White and national; in the end, it has become global. So White nationalists need to choose which camp they want to be in: that of Tradition, which includes their own Indo-European tradition, or that of modernity. Atlanticism, liberalism, and individualism are all forms of absolute evil for the Indo-European identity, since they are incompatible with it.

In his review of my book *The Fourth Political Theory*, Michael O'Meara criticized it on the grounds of advocating a return to the unrealized possibilities of the Third Political Theory. It is good that people from different camps present their responses to the Fourth Political Theory, but it uses typically old Right/Third Way racist/anti-Semitic arguments. It is not too profound, nor too hollow. I doubt that we can get anywhere by repeating the same agenda of Yockey and so on. This draws the line between the Third Way and the Fourth Way. At the same time, I consider Heidegger to be a precursor of the Fourth Political Theory, and he was acting and thinking in the context of the Third Political Theory.

Concerning the "identitarians," I have never uttered the name of Faye in all of my writing—he is not bad, but also not good. I consider Alain de Benoist to be brilliant—simply the best. Those "identitarians" who view the positive attitude toward Islam or Turks as a negative aspect of the Fourth Political Theory do so, I believe, partly due to the manipulation of globalist forces who seek to divide those revolutionary forces which are capable of challenging the liberal-capitalist Atlanticist hegemony.

Muslims form a part of the Russian population, and are an important minority. Therefore, Islamophobia implicitly calls for the break-up of Russia. The difference between Europe and Russia in our attitude toward Islam is that, for us, Muslims are an organic part of the whole, while for Europe they are a post-colonial wave of re-invaders from a different geopolitical and cultural space. But since we have a common enemy in the globalist elite, which is pro-Pussy Riot/Femen, pro-gay marriage, anti-Putin, anti-Iran, anti- Chávez, anti-social justice, and so on, we all need to develop a common strategy with the Muslims. Our traditions are quite different, but the anti-traditional world that is attacking us is united, and so must we become.

If "identitarians" really love their identity, they should ally themselves with the Eurasianists, alongside the traditionalists and the enemies of capitalism belonging to any people, religion, culture, or political camp. Being anti-Communist, anti-Muslim, anti-Eastern, pro-American, or Atlanticist today means to belong to the other side. It means to be on the side of the current global order and its financial oligarchy. But that is illogical, because the globalists are in the process of destroying any identity except for that of the individual, and to forge an alliance with them therefore means to betray the essence of one's cultural identity.

The problem with the Left is different. It is good when it opposes the capitalist order, but it lacks a spiritual dimension. The Left usually represents itself as an alternative path to modernization, and in doing so it also opposes organic values, traditions and religion, just as liberalism does.

I would be happy to see Left-wing identitarians who defend social justice while attacking capitalism on one hand, and who embrace spiritual Tradition and attack modernity on the other. There is only one enemy: the global, liberal capitalist order supported by North American hegemony (which is also directed against the genuine American identity).

In terms of traditionalism, usually traditionalism is defensive or is considered to be such. What we need is to break this assumption and promote offensive traditionalism. We should attack (hyper)modernity and make the status quo explode, in the name of the Return. I mean "offensive" in all ways. We need to insist.

Politics is the instrument of modernity. I think neo-Gramsciism is an important tool. We have to form a historic bloc of traditionalists alongside organic intellectuals of a new type. We have Orthodox Christians (and perhaps other types of Christians as well), Muslims, Buddhists, and Hindus who all reject the idea of the "Lockean heartland" (as per Kees van der Pijl) becoming global. We need to attack it together, not by ourselves. And we need to attack in any possible way — everyone as he or she is able — physically, politically, and intellectually...

It is time to be offensive.

Soon the world will descend into chaos. The financial system is going to collapse. Disorder, ethnic, and social conflicts will be breaking out everywhere. Europe is doomed. Asia is in tumult. The oceans of immigrants everywhere will overthrow the existing order. The present system will be broken and disbanded.

After this transitional period, direct global dictatorship will be implemented. We should be prepared and start to organize the global resistance right now — the planetary network of traditionalists, Conservative Revolutionaries, Heideggerians, the partisans of the Fourth Political Theory and multipolarity, and non-conformists of all sorts — a kind of Sacred Front beyond Right and Left, and consisting of different, older political and ideological taxonomies. All three of the political theories have been phased out of modernity, and also out of conventional and assumed history. We, and also our enemies, are entering absolutely new ground.

Every traditionalist should ask himself (or herself) the following questions:

1. Why have I arrived to be on the side of Tradition in opposition to modernity?

2. What is the reality that makes me what I am, in essence? Where have I got it from?

3. Is my vocation as a traditionalist the result of my socio-cultural heritage (society, family, and culture) or is it the result of some other factor?

4. How it is possible, in the midst of modernity and postmodernity, to be differentiated from them?

5. In which way can I cause the modern world around me real damage? (In other words, how can I effectively fight against the Devil?)

The Fourth Political Theory struggles for the cause of all peoples, but it is not made for the people. It is a call to the intellectual elite of every human society, and rejects hegemony in all senses (philosophical, social, and political). This time, the people cannot help us. This time, we must help the people.

Opposing us is nothing more than an intellectual elite, but it is a hegemonic one. All its material power is nothing but an illusion and a phantasm: its texts, discourse, and words are what really counts. Its force lays in its thought. And it is on the level of thought that we have to fight and, finally, win. Everything material that opposes us is actually nothing but pure privation. Only thought really exists.

It is easy to manipulate the masses, much easier than to persuade the few. Quantity is the enemy of quality — the more so, the worse. The capitalist elite thinks differently. That error will be fatal. For them. And we are going to prove it.

We need an open, undogmatic Front that is beyond Right and Left.

We have prepared for the coming moment of opportunity for too long. But now, finally, it is not so far in the future.

We will change the course of history. At present, it is on a very wrong course.

We can only win if we combine our efforts.

If You are in Favor of Global Liberal Hegemony, You are the Enemy

Interview with Alexander Dugin in New Delhi, India, 19 February 2012

In February 2012, Professor Dugin travelled to New Delhi, India to attend the 40th World Congress of the International Institute of Sociology, the theme of which was 'After Western Hegemony: Social Science and its Publics'. Prof. Dugin was kind enough to take some time away from the conference to answer a few questions by representatives of Arktos who attended the event. The interview was conducted by Daniel Friberg, CEO of Arktos, and John B. Morgan, Editor-in-Chief.

There is a perception in the West that you are a Russian nationalist. Do you identify with that description?

The concept of the nation is a capitalist, Western one. On the other hand, Eurasianism appeals to cultural and ethnic differences, and not unification on the basis of the individual, as nationalism presumes. Ours differs from nationalism because we defend a pluralism of values. We are defending ideas, not our community; ideas, not our society. We are challenging postmodernity, but not on behalf of the Russian nation alone. Postmodernity is a yawning abyss. Russia is only one part of this global struggle. It is certainly an important part, but not the ultimate goal. For those of us in Russia, we can't save it without saving the world at the same time. And likewise, we can't save the world without saving Russia.

It is not only a struggle against Western universalism. It is a struggle against all universalisms, even Islamic ones. We cannot accept any desire to impose any universalism upon others — neither Western, Islamic, socialist, liberal, or Russian. We defend not Russian imperialism or revanchism, but rather a global vision and multipolarity based on the dialectic of civilization. Those we oppose say that the multiplicity of civilizations necessarily implies a clash. This is a false assertion.

Globalisation and American hegemony bring about a bloody intrusion and trigger violence between civilizations where there could be peace, dialogue or conflict, depending on historical circumstances. But imposing a hidden hegemony implies conflict and, inevitably, worse in the future. So they say peace but they make war. We defend justice — not peace or war, but justice and dialogue and the natural right of any culture to maintain its identity and to pursue what it wants to be. Not only historically, as in multiculturalism, but also in the future. We must free ourselves from these pretend universalisms.

What do you think Russia's role will be in organizing the anti-modern forces?

There are different levels involved in the creation of anti-globalist, or rather anti-Western, movements and currents around the world. The basic idea is to unite the people who are fighting against the status quo. So, what is the status quo? It is a series of connected phenomena bringing about an important shift from modernity to post-modernity. It is shaped by a shift from the unipolar world, represented primarily by the influence of the United States and Western Europe, to so-called non-polarity as exemplified by today's implicit hegemony and those revolutions that have been orchestrated by it through proxy, as for example the various Orange revolutions. The basic intent behind this strategy is for the West to eventually control the planet, not only through direct intervention, but also via the universalization of its set of values, norms and ethics.

The status quo of the West's liberal hegemony has become global. It is a Westernization of all of humanity. This means that its norms, such as the free market, free trade, liberalism, parliamentarian democracy, human rights and absolute individualism, have become universal. This set of norms is interpreted differently in the various regions of the world, but the West regards its specific interpretation as being both self-evident and its universalization as inevitable. This is nothing less than a colonization of the spirit and of the mind. It is a new kind of colonialism, a new kind of power, and a new kind of control that is put into effect through a network. Everyone who is connected to the global network becomes subjected to its code. It is part of the postmodern West, and is rapidly becoming global. The price a nation or a people has to pay to become connected to the West's globalization network is acceptance of these norms. It is the West's new hegemony. It is a migration from the open hegemony of the West, as represented by the colonialism and outright imperialism of the past, to an implicit, more subtle version.

To fight this global threat to humanity, it is important to unite all the various forces that would, in earlier times, have been called anti-imperialist. In this age, we should better understand our enemy. The enemy of today is hidden. It acts by exploiting the norms and values of the Western path of development and ignoring the plurality represented by other cultures and civilizations. Today, we invite all who insist on the worth of the specific values of non-Western civilizations, and where other forms of values exist, to challenge this attempt at a global universalization and its hidden hegemony.

This is a cultural, philosophical, ontological, and eschatological struggle, because in the status quo we identify the essence of the Dark Age, or the great paradigm. But we should also move from a purely theoretical stance to a practical, geopolitical level. And at this geopolitical level, Russia preserves the potential, resources, and inclination to confront this challenge, because Russian history has long been intuitively oriented against the same horizon. Russia is a great power where there is an acute awareness of what is going on in the world, historically speaking, and which possesses a deep consciousness of its own eschatological mission. Therefore it is only natural that Russia should play a central part in this anti-status quo coalition. Russia defended its identity against Catholicism, Protestantism, and the modern West during Tsarist times, and then against liberal capitalism during Soviet times. Now there is a third wave of this struggle — the struggle against postmodernity, ultra-liberalism and globalization. But this time, Russia is no longer able to rely on its own resources. It cannot fight solely under the banner of Orthodox Christianity. Nor is reintroducing or relying on Marxist doctrine a viable option, since Marxism is in itself a major root of the destructive ideas constituting postmodernity.

Russia is now one of many participants in this global struggle, and cannot fight this war alone. We need to unite all the forces that are opposed to Western norms and its economic system. So we need to make alliances with all the Leftist social and political movements that challenge the status quo of liberal capitalism. We should likewise ally ourselves with all identitarian forces in any culture that refuse globalism for cultural reasons. From this perspective, Islamic movements, Hindu movements or nationalist movements from all over the world should also be regarded as allies. Hindus, Buddhists, Christians, and pagan identitarians in Europe, America or Latin America, or other types of cultures, should all form a common front. The idea is to unite all of them, struggling against the single enemy and the singular evil for a multiplicity of ideas about what is good.

What we are against will unite us, while what we are in favor of divides us. Therefore, we should emphasize what we oppose. The common enemy unites us, while the positive values each of us are defending actually divides us. Therefore, we must create strategic alliances to overthrow the present order of things, of which the core could be described as human rights, anti-hierarchy, and political correctness — everything that is the face of the Beast, the anti-Christ or, in other terms, Kali-Yuga.

Where does traditionalist spirituality fit into the Eurasian agenda?

There are secularized cultures, but at the core of all of them, the spirit of Tradition remains, religious or otherwise. By defending the multiplicity, plurality and polycentrism of cultures, we are making an appeal to the principles of their essences, which we can only find in the spiritual traditions. But we try to link this attitude to the necessity for social justice and the freedom of differing societies in the hope for better political regimes. The idea is to join the spirit of Tradition with the desire for social justice. And we don't want to oppose them, because that is the main strategy of hegemonic power: to divide Left and Right, to divide cultures, to divide ethnic groups, East and West, Muslims and Christians. We invite Right and Left to unite, and not to oppose traditionalism and spirituality, social justice and social dynamism. So we are not on the Right or on the Left. We are against liberal postmodernity. Our idea is to join all the fronts and not let them divide us. When we stay divided, they can rule us safely. If we are united, their rule will immediately end. That is our global strategy. And when we try to join the spiritual traditions with social justice, there is an immediate panic among liberals. They fear this very much.

Which spiritual tradition should someone who wishes to participate in the Eurasianist struggle adopt, and is this a necessary component?

One should seek to become a concrete part of the society in which one lives, and follow the tradition that prevails there. For example, I am Russian Orthodox. This is my tradition. Under different conditions, however, some individuals might choose a different spiritual path. What is important is to have roots. There is no universal answer. If someone neglects this spiritual basis, but is willing to take part in our struggle, during the struggle he may well find some deeper spiritual meaning. Our idea is that our enemy is deeper than the merely human. Evil is deeper than humanity, greed, or exploitation. Those who fight on behalf of evil are those who have no spiritual faith. Those who oppose it may encounter it. Or, perhaps not. It is an open question — it is not obligatory. It is advisable, but not necessary.

What do you think of the European New Right and Julius Evola, and in particular, their respective opposition to Christianity?

It is up to the Europeans to decide which kind of spirituality to revive. For us Russians, it is Orthodox Christianity. We regard our tradition as being authentic. We see our tradition as being a continuation of the earlier, pre-Christian traditions of Russia, as is reflected in our veneration of the saints and icons, among other aspects. Therefore, there is no opposition between our earlier and later traditions. Evola opposes the Christian tradition of the West. What is interesting is his critique of the desacralization of Western Christianity. This fits well with the Orthodox critique of Western Christianity. It is easy to see that the secularization of Western Christianity gives us liberalism. The secularization of the Orthodox religion gives us Communism. It is individualism versus collectivism. For us, the problem is not with Christianity itself, as it is in the West.

Evola made an attempt to restore Tradition. The New Right also tries to restore the Western tradition, which is very good. But being Russian Orthodox, I cannot decide which is the right path for Europe to take, since we have a different set of values. We don't want to tell the Europeans what to do, nor do we want to be told what to do by the Europeans. As Eurasianists, we'll accept any solution. Since Evola was European, he could discuss and propose the proper solution for Europe. Each of us can only state our personal opinion. But I have found that we have more in common with the New Right than with the Catholics. I share many of the same views as Alain de Benoist. I consider him to be the foremost intellectual in Europe today. That it is not the case with modern Catholics. They wish to convert Russia, and that is not compatible with our plans. The New Right does not want to impose European paganism upon others. I also consider Evola to be a master and a symbolic figure of the final revolt and the great revival, as well as Guénon. For me, these two individuals are the essence of the Western tradition in this Dark Age.

In an earlier conversation, you mentioned that Eurasianists should work with some jihadist groups. However, they tend to be universalist, and their stated goal is the imposition of Islamic rule over the entire world. What are the prospects for making such a coalition work?

Jihadis are universalists, just as secular Westerners who seek globalization are. But they are not the same, because the Western project seeks to dominate all the others and impose its hegemony everywhere. It attacks us directly every day through the global media, in the realm of fashion, by setting examples for youth, and so on. We are submerged in this global cultural hegemony. Salafist universalism is a kind of marginal alternative. They should not be thought of in the same way as those who seek globalization. They also fight against our enemy. We don't like any universalists, but there are universalists who attack us today and win, and there are also non-conformist universalists who are fighting against the hegemony of the Western, liberal universalists, and therefore they are tactical friends for the time being. Before their project of a global Islamic state can be realized, we will have many battles and conflicts. And global liberal domination is a fact. We therefore invite everybody to fight alongside us against this hegemony and this status quo. I prefer to discuss what is the reality at present, rather than what may exist in the future. All those who oppose liberal hegemony are our friends for the moment. This is not morality, it is strategy. Carl Schmitt said that politics begins by distinguishing between friends and enemies. There are no eternal friends and no eternal enemies. We are struggling against the existing universal hegemony. Everyone fights against it for their own particular set of values.

For the sake of coherence we should also prolong, widen, and create a broader alliance. I don't like Salafists. It would be much better to align with traditionalist Sufis, for example. But I prefer working with the Salafists against the common enemy than to waste energy in fighting against them while ignoring the greater threat.

If you are in favor of global liberal hegemony, you are the enemy. If you are against it, you are a friend. The first is inclined to accept this hegemony; the other is in revolt.

In light of recent events in Libya, what are your personal views of Gaddafi?

President Medvedev committed a real crime against Gaddafi and helped to initiate a chain of interventions in the Arab world. It was a real crime committed by our President. His hands are bloodied. He is a collaborator with the West. The crime of murdering Gaddafi was partly his responsibility. We Eurasianists defended Gaddafi, not because we were fans or supporters of him or his *Green Book*, but because it was a matter of principles. Behind the insurgency in Libya was Western hegemony, and it imposed bloody chaos. When Gaddafi fell, Western hegemony grew stronger. It was our defeat. But not the final one. This war has many episodes. We lost the battle, but not the war. And perhaps something different will emerge in Libya, because the situation is quite unstable. For example, the Iraq War actually strengthened Iran's influence in the region, contrary to the designs of the Western hegemonists.

Given the situation in Syria at present, the scenario is repeating itself. However, this situation, with Putin returning to power, is in a much better position. At least he is consistent in his support for President al-Assad. Perhaps this will not be enough to stop Western intervention in Syria. I suggest that Russia assist our ally more effectively by supplying weapons, financing, and so forth. The fall of Libya was a defeat for Russia. The fall of Syria will be yet another failure.

What is your opinion of, and relationship to Vladimir Putin?

He was much better than Yeltsin. He saved Russia from a complete crash in the 1990s. Russia was on the verge of disaster. Before Putin, Western-style liberals were in a position to dictate politics in Russia. Putin restored the sovereignty of the Russian state. That is the reason why I became his supporter. However, by 2003, Putin stopped his patriotic, Eurasianist reforms, putting aside the development of a genuine national strategy, and began to accommodate the economic liberals who wanted Russia to become a part of the project of globalization. As a result, he began to lose legitimacy, and so I became more and more critical of him. In some circumstances I worked with people around him to support him in some of his policies, while I opposed him in others. When Medvedev was chosen as his heir, it was a catastrophe, since the people positioned around him were all liberals. I was against Medvedev. I opposed him, in part, from the Eurasianist point-of-view.

Now Putin will return. All the liberals are against him, and all the pro-Western forces are against him. But he himself has not yet made his attitude toward this clear. However, he is obliged to win the support of the Russian people anew. It is impossible to continue otherwise. He is in a critical situation, although he doesn't seem to understand this. He is hesitating to choose the patriotic side. He thinks he can find support among some of the liberals, which is completely false. Nowadays,

I am not so critical of him as I was before, but I think he is in a critical situation. If he continues to hesitate, he will fail. I recently published a book, *Putin Vs Putin* (English edition: Arktos, 2014), because his greatest enemy is himself. Because he is hesitating, he is losing more and more popular support. The Russian people feel deceived by him. He may be a kind of authoritarian leader without authoritarian charisma. I've cooperated with him in some cases, and opposed him on others. I am in contact with him. But there are so many forces around him. The liberals and the Russian patriots around him are not so brilliant, intellectually speaking. Therefore, he is obliged to rely only upon himself and his intuition. But intuition cannot be the only source of political decision-making and strategy. When he returns to power, he will be pushed to return to his earlier anti-Western policies, because our society is anti-Western in nature. Russia has a long tradition of rebellion against foreign invaders, and of helping others who resist injustice, and the Russian people view the world through this lens. They will not be satisfied with a ruler who does not govern in keeping with this tradition.

Other Books Published by Arktos

The Dharma Manifesto
by Sri Dharma Pravartaka Acharya

Beyond Human Rights
by Alain de Benoist

Carl Schmitt Today
by Alain de Benoist

Manifesto for a European Renaissance
by Alain de Benoist & Charles Champetier

The Problem of Democracy
by Alain de Benoist

Germany's Third Empire
by Arthur Moeller van den Bruck

The Arctic Home in the Vedas
by Bal Gangadhar Tilak

Revolution from Above
by Kerry Bolton

The Fourth Political Theory
by Alexander Dugin

Putin vs Putin
by Alexander Dugin

Return of the Swastika
by Koenraad Elst

Fascism Viewed from the Right
by Julius Evola

Metaphysics of War
by Julius Evola

Notes on the Third Reich
by Julius Evola

The Path of Cinnabar
by Julius Evola

Archeofuturism
by Guillaume Faye

Convergence of Catastrophes
by Guillaume Faye

Sex and Deviance
by Guillaume Faye

Why We Fight
by Guillaume Faye

Suprahumanism
by Daniel S. Forrest

The WASP Question
by Andrew Fraser

We are Generation Identity
by Génération Identitaire

War and Democracy
by Paul Gottfried

The Saga of the Aryan Race
by Porus Homi Havewala

The Owls of Afrasiab
by Lars Holger Holm

Homo Maximus
by Lars Holger Holm

De Naturae Natura
by Alexander Jacob

Fighting for the Essence
by Pierre Krebs

Can Life Prevail?
by Pentti Linkola

The Conservative
by H. P. Lovecraft

The NRA and the Media
by Brian Anse Patrick

Rise of the Anti-Media
by Brian Anse Patrick

The Ten Commandments of Propaganda
by Brian Anse Patrick

Zombology
by Brian Anse Patrick

Morning Crafts
by Tito Perdue

A Handbook of Traditional Living
by Raido

The Agni and the Ecstasy
by Steven J. Rosen

The Jedi in the Lotus
by Steven J. Rosen

Barbarians
by Richard Rudgley

Wildest Dreams
by Richard Rudgley

Essential Substances
by Richard Rudgley

It Cannot Be Stormed
by Ernst von Salomon

Tradition & Revolution
by Troy Southgate

Against Democracy and Equality
by Tomislav Sunic

Defining Terrorism
by Abir Taha

Nietzsche's Coming God
by Abir Taha

Verses of Light
by Abir Taha

A Europe of Nations
by Markus Willinger

Generation Identity
by Markus Willinger

The Initiate: Journal of Traditional Studies
by David J. Wingfield (ed.)

CPSIA information can be obtained
at www.ICGtesting.com
Printed in the USA
BVHW03s0718220918
528243BV00001B/73/P